I0784070

The Right Word

SELECTED WRITINGS
LITERARY CLUB OF CINCINNATI

2025

FIRST EDITION

2025 Praus Press

All rights reserved. No part of this book may be reproduced or transmitted in any form or by any means graphic, electronic or mechanical, including photocopying, recording, taping or by any information storage or retrieval system, without the permission in writing from the publisher.

Published by Praus Press

CONTENTS

INTRODUCTION

Tools of the trade—artists have their palettes and easels, sculptors their chisels and knives, but writers? Their tool kit is that cornucopia of words, overflowing in richness yet ever so challenging in the care and precision it demands of those who dare employ them

This latest volume of works by members of The Literary Club offers examples of the beauty, the power and sheer magic of words artfully crafted. On display are stories and poems reflecting the labors of a group of club members embarked on that elusive search for the right word to express their thoughts and ideas. One of the essayists even wonders whether finding the right one is indeed an impossible task.

Leading off the collection is a poetic set of meditations on words by the club's unofficial poet laureate, Richard Hague. Then readers are taken on literary adventures by others—to an eatery called Irk's, to a classroom encounter with mud, to a soiree with Madame X, and much more. Finally, we dip into the club's archives, now spanning 175 years of writing, for some words about celebrated writers who should have been enrolled in our membership but somehow weren't.

We hope that readers of this volume will savor the outpouring of words as much as those did who assembled them.

WILLIAM BURLEIGH joined his hometown newspaper staff at age 14 and spent more than a half century in journalism jobs, ending as chairman of the E.W. Scripps Company, America's oldest media chain. In another association he cherishes, Bill joined The Literary Club in 1978 and was privileged to serve as its president in 2001-02.

Instructions

Beyond the initial difficulty, which is "What word?" there is nothing impossible. Approach the task with confidence and equanimity; wear nice clothes, not too tight, and remember your p's and q's. Naturally, you may want to rehearse, but sadly, that is forbidden. You may say the word only once, and once you have said it, it is forever forbidden to repeat yourself. In this way, the evolution of the tongue is assured. In this way, the evolution of the tongue is assured: you may say the word only once, and once you have said it, it is forever forbidden to repeat yourself. Naturally, you may want to rehearse, but sadly, that is forbidden. Approach the task with confidence and equanimity; wear nice clothes, not too tight, and remember your p's and q's. Beyond the initial difficulty, which is "What word?" there is nothing impossible.

– RICHARD HAGUE

Lafcadio Hearn

1

from Anniversaries And Neglected Men

OCTOBER 30, 1978

ESLIE ASBURY

Even in the last century when flowery oratory was the fashion, all official participants read their offerings and left a copy, a club rule which discourages prolixity, interpolations, and "terminological inexactitude" (a euphemism coined by Winston Churchill to call his opponents ignoramuses or liars.) An exception was Ainsworth F. Spofford's historic speech on our fiftieth anniversary.

This was the largest club meeting. All former members were invited and 52 came, mostly from long distances. 84 active members and six guests made a total of 142 present at the 50th dinner, which was the longest, the eight-speech program lasting until midnight. The heroes of the evening were three of the four living men who were elected during the first Club year—*ad hoc* President J. W. Herron, Henry Blackwell of Boston, who wrote a poem for the occasion; and Ainsworth F. Spofford, director of the Library of Congress for 40 years, who made the principal address.

Lucius Hine, the fourth surviving first-year member, was not invited. In 1877, he had been indicted for publishing treasonous statements about the President and the government and, though pardoned by President Hayes, he was in Club disgrace. Hine was then the only survivor of four internationally known radical socialist agitators who were members of the Club. The others were J.B. Stallo, Moncure Conway and August Willich, the only card-carrying Communist member of the Club.

Among the guests was Dr. Edward Ayers, the President of the University of Cincinnati, who made one of the eight speeches. Later, Louis More, the new professor of physics, proposed him for membership but he failed of election, the only president of the university ever turned down by the Club. In cleaning out the faculty, Dr. Ayers had not fired any Club members, but he had fired several of their incompetent friends. Four famous members of the Club—John Uri Lloyd, James Albert Green, Rabbi Phlipson, and E.W. Coy, who opposed Dr. Ayer and even headed a citizens committee to protect the firings — never forgave themselves for their mistake. Dr. Ayers replaced the incompetents with such men as Professors D.T. More, Max Bell, Charles F. Hicks and other who became outstanding on the faculty and members of the Literary Club.

Dr. Ayers was a martyr to politics, but the controversy taught Boss Cox and all later politicians never to let self-seeking doctors or others talk them into intervening in the affairs of the university.

On the whole, no club has been as free of personal of political bias in selecting members. Confident of its proven ability to absorb able eccentrics, the Club has pursued diversity even to extremism. However, it has been guilty of several known acts of deliberate omission or neglect, some pardonable and all understandable, if not justifiable. In addition to Dr. Ayers, I often heard old members regret that Lafcadio Hearn and George Pendleton were not elected.

Lafcadio Hearn lived in Cincinnati for eight years. As a child, he lost one eye due to an injury, and the other one over-developed, giving him a grotesque look, hindering his social acceptability, but goading him to prove himself. People who are normal physically and emotionally seldom develop latent genius. They are too popular and too engrossed in routine affairs. They believe the Declaration of Independence, which says that everyone is entitled to the pursuit of happiness. This is bad advice. The direct pursuit of riches or happiness is a delusion, leading at best to successful mediocrity. The true road is the pursuit of perfection which may even bring riches, always brings satisfaction and sometimes brings lasting fame. Lafcadio Hearn sought perfection. Shunned by many, he was at first anti-social, but his genius was discovered by Frank Duveneck, who got him out of the waterfront dives, induced Murat Halstead to start him on the old *Commercial* for which he wrote sensational stories, and, with his later accomplishments, was probably the most brilliant writer to live in Cincinnati. Duveneck and Halstead were members of the Club, but they never proposed him for membership, nor even brought him to an anniversary dinner.

George Pendleton, Congressman and U.S Senator, the father of civil service legislation, was the only Cincinnati Democrat except Judson Harmon (a reformed Republican and a member of the Club) to achieve national stature in politics. That Pendleton was a Democrat, they could forgive, but, as Mr. Wiley said, the "union at any cost" veterans never forgave Pendleton and McClellan for running against Lincoln on a "peace at any price" platform.

If we ever create a posthumous membership list to include great Cincinnatians who were not elected to the Club, each member will have his favorites. Mine would be Howard Ayers, Lafcadio Hearn and George Pendleton.

DR. ESLIE ASBURY was born in 1895 in rural Central Kentucky. Attending the University of Cincinnati where he received a Bachelor of Science degree, graduating thereafter from the College of Medicine in 1920. His post-graduate medical training was done in general and orthopedic surgery at the Mayo Clinic. In 1930, he was the youngest ever physician to be elected chief-of-staff of the Good Samaritan Hospital.

Asbury was elected to the Literary Club of Cincinnati in 1926, serving as the club's historian. Over the years, Dr. Asbury was one of its most prolific writers and active members.

Another important phase of his life began with the purchase of a horse farm in Nicholas County, Kentucky. By the late 1940s, yearlings from his farm, Forest Retreat, included several thoroughbred champions being bred there, including the 1954 Kentucky Derby winner, Determine.

He was a founding member of the Keeneland Association in 1936, the founder of the Ohio Valley Thoroughbred Club, and a member of the board of trustees of Keeneland since its inception. He was one of the first members elected to The Jockey Club who did not live on the Eastern Seaboard and was an honored guest of the Thoroughbred Club of America.

Honored as a Great Living Cincinnatian in 1981, , Dr. Asbury died on September 4, 1988 at age 93.

2

Dancing with Satan's Daughter

GORDON CHRISTENSON

After ten thousand years of flying, Archangel Lucifer—cast-out son of the morning, elder brother, and noble loser of the war in heaven—is now the monstrous Satan. He falls into the abyss, frightened and alone in Dante's hell."

And Then There Was Night—Dying

"Hell is eternal absence," Satan cries from the dark. "Hell is loving: It is saying: Alas! So, where is she, my light? Where is my light and luminosity? . . . The vast darkness fills me with its ecstasy, god is dying to me, and I feel in my heart the strange and wild plentitude of night. I shout, joyful, triumphant, restless ... I shall bite the soul. I am the hooded executioner. God shall die ... my flames, dancing beneath the universe, shall set him ablaze ... I am evil; I am night; I am terror.

Birthing of the Angel Liberty

A fire in the down of a white feather that escaped from Satan's rebellious wing made it shiver. Once it was part of the wing, beating day and night with atheist mendacity. In flight, the feather felt majesty and madness. Now separated from the wing, as if from a dark womb, the feather, shone, pulsated, grew, took shape, came alive, and seemed a splendor transformed into a woman ...standing erect, lighting infinity with her innocent smile. Her face, melding the flame with brilliance, blazed, defying the engulfing abyss. Beneath a charming brow, flashed a dance of lightning in the eye of Dawn.

And so it was that from this pure white feather from the wing of the monster archangel Satan, a new angel is born. Satan has birthed a daughter—stunningly innocent, delicate, exquisite!

Might we say it is the birth of tragedy? Possibly, but she is redeemed from tragedy through Thunder, Perfect Mind, a Nag Hammadi poem of divine feminine power that unites all opposites.

Oh Lord, what shall we call this angel? In the Absolute, where Being dwells, a word, the Spirit of Logos, dances upon the brow of this magnificent, young angel, still floating in the vast light.3 It's a name, Liberty! Her name—mythical, within the aura of Sophia, consort of the Infinite Spirit, and god's wise agent of creation.

I'm Pheuth'—spelled p, h, e, u, t, h, apostrophe. Pronounced fee-youth. I'm a cat. Who else has my name? What other feral white cat writes poems? I'm an anarchist, consecrated in the early fifties by two young college friends out of nothing but their imaginations.

They invented me from an archetype of a feral cat—nihilistic, haughty, and cunning—named Pheuth'. These guys thought the name hilarious, and apt.

Why? Am I not real? I was furious! They mocked my dignity; insulted my pride! They left me on my own. I prowled the dark in the unconscious where I preyed on hapless dogs, birds, bunnies. My fury only got worse.

One of the two guys died recently of Alzheimer's. He was a distinguished professor of Heideggerian philosophy who feigned fascism.

The other is a law professor now and a complete fraud and con-artist. He pretends to be an amateur poet who hates to dance. He is mistaken. Everything dances—beetles, bees, butterflies, trees, slaves, Persian princes, Irish cleaning ladies—Zarathustra dances on a tight rope over the marketplace. Football players dance to celebrate touchdowns.

This guy pretends to know something about the law. Who does he think he is? He ought not laugh at his creations. He is my creator and yet vomits dreck about me from his unconscious into his knowing self. I swore I'd get even, but that was a long time ago.

Someday, when he's more aware, I'll do him in. For now, I must bide my time.

Listen! I hear a strange sound: "Gilgamesh is dead!" Ah! It's from Lilith. She's coming up from the underworld. I've dealt with her before.

What's she saying? That we all will die? Big deal. So what? Gilgamesh learned the hard way. And you, Lilith! You would kill him?

Lilith
You heard right., Pheuth'. . . Yes, if I kill Gilgamesh, I won't ever die! He was a hero king who killed powerful men and feared women like the goddess Ishtar. He turned down her offer to be his lover and then was scared of her punishment of death to take revenge. He was afraid of death, and he's afraid of me now. He sought to be immortal like the gods and never die. Even his shadow is afraid of me.

Lilith calls down. Gilgamesh, why didn't you ask the goddess Ishtar to dance before rejecting her? She would have taken you more seriously than Zeus ever would. Promises of eternal life without death are false! But any goddess loves to dance, even in the darkest part of the abyss. What never dies is dancing, which is eternal. To dance is to live.

Let me remind your shadow of the palace relief, now in Paris at the Louvre. It tells your story, about the time writing first developed in the 7th or 8th century BCE. Your right hand grasps a snake of daemonic sexual power by its head. That's me, Lilith, Gilgamesh is choking. He wants me to die.

Your left arm is around the neck of a lion to break its natural power superior to your own as king.

You see, I'm Adam's first wife and Eve's big sister. I am the demon-dancer, Priestess of the night.

I am the sacred whore in the gateway of the Temple; Mother to the motherless; nemesis of Satan's oh so pure a daughter, Liberty.

My sexual fire is too hot.

I am Lilith, now living in the shadows under the hill, loving to hear Liturgy for Lilith, waiting for you, Pheuth' The cat's haunches are ready. The tip of his tail twitches.

We have much in common!

There was an old woman lived under the hill And if she's not gone, she lives there still. Suddenly, Pheuth' pounces onto Lilith with the feral virility of a male cat on the make. Lilith shoves him aside. You're too horny, pal. Cool down. This leap is the Devil's and brings violence and meanness. It's unnatural. A cat dance with the Spirit is more in keeping with your reputation and savoir faire, the kind holy whores like me enjoy.!

To Live One Must Die

To die in order to live becomes much clearer in earth time when encountering Gustav Mahler's Resurrection Symphony. Two soloists, a huge choir of 180, and orchestra of 110 members, enter Jesus-the-Nazarene's shadow of death—to die suffering the cross so that life can be lived.

In the first half of the performance, the orchestra's brassy tumult in the world, with discordant noise from the timpani, buries the strings' faint sweet songs. Then toward the last movement, a solitary human voice of the soprano pierces the helter-skelter. Throughout the performance, the entire chorus sat frozen in silence, magnificently restrained, not yet joining the soprano's pure lament. We are fixated on this chorus, wondering when it will awaken. In the daze of twilight in the dawn, it finds itself moving and humming in the chaos of the underworld—growing louder and brighter until the light becomes a fierce human cry:

Chorus—"What was created must pass away! / What has passed away must rise! / Cease trembling! / Prepare yourself to live!"

Chorus stands up singing—"I shall die in order to live!

Soloists and Chorus join—"Rise again, yes you will rise again, /my heart, in the twinkling of an eye!"

Then in swelling crescendo, soloists and chorus all stand up, singing with the full orchestra playing, louder than the sound of light to fill every nook in Music Hall. From Hades' pit, the vicious dog enters to yelp and explode with timpani, strings, horns, and brass, as if from hell. Human voices cry from the world outside the Hall, but not a breath can be heard inside. The conductor's baton holds the orchestra and audience in suspense. Reaching perfect silence, the baton moves the orchestra to its sublime conclusion, keeping the suspense The conductor slowly lowers his baton in the final step of the dance into silence. A faint flick of the baton, and it is the end.

Finis! The audience explodes, rising in shouts and applause. Finis! Finis!!

Civilization is about to run its course, too.

End of a Civilization—A Dark Age Follows
The end of a civilization of Homo sapiens, the most violent and destructive of all human species within the last ten thousand years, happened as recently as the late Bronze Age.

In 1177 B.C.E., an advanced civilization of world trade collapsed. Its vast network was headed by male Pharoahs, kings and emperors of great wealth from Egypt, the Hittite and the Canaanite empires in commerce across the Aegean and Eastern Mediterranean city-states. Our classical archeologist Jack Davis wrote that" the world they had known for more than three centuries suddenly collapsed and essentially vanished."

Marauding "Sea People"—victims perhaps more than oppressors—aided by internal upheavals were thought to have been the main cause. A dark age of three to four hundred years followed the destruction of global trading. During the long era of decline, slowly, a radically changed cosmopolitan civilization begins to emerge.

The cultural residue, shaky from the Greeks and Semites, grapple with decline among themselves. Impoverished from all the wars and chaos of ancient times and barely surviving, they demand a powerful one or many gods all through the dark age to rescue them. Just as civil conflicts between warring factions in Caesar!s Rome later were rendering the old Republican Senate impotent, a structure of kings and imperators with divine moorings in reason seemed destined to rise again to roars from hungry and rudderless mobs dancing to different gods in the dusty roads and ruins of surviving ancient cities.

Living Lords of the Dance

In Babylonian legend, at the beginning, the god Apus and the goddess Tiamat danced to separate a mystical god Marduk from the chaos of swirls of water. He first slew the dragon of chaos, then birthed the gods, and finally created the universe and humankind.

In this alive, orderly cosmos, the gods created an eternal paradise of goodness in a garden with the tree of knowledge of Good and Evil for Adam and the first sisters Lilith and Eve. Early writers—of Persian, Arabian, Greek and Hebraic literatures brought widespread mythologies of dance: The Hindu Lord of the Dance legend from Nataraja; Sanskrit as balance or harmony; the Torah as goodness; god's creation as "very good"; poetry of Persian Rimi as the dancing soul that lives within; the Quran as divine sparkle of the Prophet's Suras; and the twinkling, dancing tales of the Arabian The Thousand Nights and One Night.

The Lord of the Dance

Dance, then, wherever you may be, I am the Lord of the dance, said he,

And I'll lead you all, wherever you may be,

Lilith wants to restore a matriarchal universe where the good news also contains evil, violence, absurdity, ecstatic frenzy, and meaninglessness. Etched into developing primal brains, is the folktale of survival and a dread of suffocating, of losing the breath of life, of being subordinate to the first man Adam when she was created equal to him and the first sister to Eve.

When Lilith, Adam's first wife , talked the serpent into beguiling Eve, Adam's second, sweeter wife, he divorced Lilith and she flew away on wings of her freedom, morphing into demon harlot, a Temple whore, a succubus—demon in female form who has sex with men in their sleep.

We evolved, each of us, beginning from the instant of birthing of the Universe in the big bang nearly 14 billion years ago inside a biosphere of our remote home, planet earth, which itself evolved uniquely, taking up four or five billion years—not thousands—from an infusion of life-stuff passed on from the evolving outer cosmos—carbon, oxygen, hydrogen, calcium molecules. These relatively recent scientific discoveries were brought into our awareness by the powerful Hubble, the Planck, the Kepler and other more recent inner and outer space telescopes. Hubble captures amazing digital images of exploding galaxies and nebulae, the birth and death of stars, the formation of solar systems, all in magnificent color. We might imagine further a finer matter of Spirit dancing in the great beyond, as stars and galaxies evolve from black holes and birthing explosions, like metaphoric incarnations.

Some scientists recently reported their successful creation of pantetheine, critical for metabolism in all living cells. Among experiments of laboratory creation, the question is how lifeless molecules produce living cells from simple to complex, spawning an intense controversy over the possibility of a science of birthing new particular life from no-life.

When individuated human life ends in death, and the myth of Gilgamesh says no one escapes it, there will never be birthed another consciously or unconsciously assembled "self" quite like an embryo of protein and genetic material that becomes an individual being with a highly evolving brain and capable of sexual reproduction and cooperating with others to survive.

With science and artificial intelligence, such a person can now be constructed, but without a dancing Spirit, it is a perfectly inhuman apparatchik.

Early in the twentieth century, Dr. Carl Jung had begun to explore through the human psyche the shadow-side of this question. He entered by recognizing a split in traditional Christianity over the soul: Why does the spirit soar to ecstasy in a loving god but the body sinks below the base pits of Hades and original sin of guilt for our carnal nature's lust for gold, power, and erotic sex.

The icon of a primordial snake swallowing its tail, is a mythical symbol of self destruction before a rebirth is possible. A modern depiction of the ancient ouroboros discovered by Kekule was revived in the scientific revolution—nuclear physics and quantum mechanics; pure mathematics; madness; psyches duped; and fear of Truth inone gigantic denial. Saying that god is good not evil, without more, is babble—words, words, words. Without a dancing Spirit in creating life and evil from nothing, ordinary language is meaningless.

Do Not Be Afraid, Little Lion of God

In Nikos Kazantzakis's book, *Saint Francis, Brother Leo* (companion of the saint and his scribe) dreamed he was a hermit among the great, celibate desert hermits who had given away their wealth and set up huts near ancient Thebes, Egypt. In the dream, Leo's father, an anchorite and a hermit, is dying and wants to see his son before he dies. In his dream Brother Leo hastens to his father's hut. His father draws him close and whispers," My son, we have been duped, and now it's too late!

There is no heaven, and no hell, either!"

"What is there then—chaos?"

"No, not even chaos." "But what then?" "Nothing!" . . .

Brother Leo woke up with a piercing cry. . . "Have we been duped? . . If it is true, what then?" He ran to find Brother Francis.

"Brother Francis," he cried as he found Brother Francis in his hut. "Help! Help!" Saint Francis calms him down and tells him:

When God had finally completed the creation of the world and had washed the mud off his hands, he sat down beneath one of the trees in Paradise and closed his eyes. "I am tired," he murmured. "Why shouldn't I rest for a minute or two?! He commanded sleep to visit him; but at that instant a goldfinch with red claws came, perched above Him and began to cry. "There is no rest, no peace; do not sleep" I will not allow Thee to sleep, for I am the human heart ... "What does this mean?" Asks Brother Leo "How could the heart of man speak to God so impertinently?"

Francis divined the thought and smiled:

Do not be afraid, little lion of God. Yes, man's insolence is limitless, but that is the way God created our hearts; that is what He wanted them to do—to stand up to Him and resist!"

Scribe Leo writes "I held my breath, trying to hear more. There was nothing more."

Pheuth' Returns

At this junction, in the here and now within our beloved Club, I'm on an interior road home—all in and joyful and yet with profound sorrow. Perhaps it's a last journey—dare I say adventure?—inside a negation of all external reality, beyond even solipsism of the present moment, beyond death. I've never been here before. To me, going beyond the subjectivism of internal imagination presents a nihilism that can turn a person mad like the snake eating its own tail. It is impossible for me to express any reality in plain, modern linear English. I must do poetics.

As I enter a central point in this ubiquitous reverie, the ephemeral cat, Pheuth! that we created from nothing seventy years ago, makes his move. Satan's daughter, Liberty, has taken her father back to heaven. She has redeemed him with her spirit that is pure love in a dance beyond good and evil, and has just returned when she encounters

Pheuth', coming up from a void beneath the abyss. He grabs her in his paws moving in the agile steps of a cat dance. She resists, going limp.

Pheuth' drags Liberty into the open-air. "Dance with me," he commands. He nibbles Liberty's ear; paws her neck; licks her face; feels her body and sees the fire in her eyes dim.

I'm incensed at the sight and shout, "Stop this!"

Phueth' instantly turns on me brandishing splaying claws and showing his sharp teeth. Dripping with rage, he hisses at me a line of the poem I'd long forgotten but he hadn't:

Your life is but an incorporeal hereditament, a fraud!

You don't yet understand, you dumb fraud. You are nothing. You know nothing.

You are worth nothing.

Satan's daughter Liberty says nothing, but shoves Pheuth' further away and I grab hold of her. This beautifully pure angel brushes my cheek lightly with her white wing, as we move back into the dance space. I begin a slow dance. She follows my steps and whispers, I'll live in you if you'll live in me.

Yes, say I, but in the death of stars and galaxies, I am truly nothing!

I've been part of nothing, she says, but I go wherever the dance may be or not be. And leaving me with a wave, she flies off with her new bright, white-feathered wings, taking her nemesis Lilith along with her and leaving Phueth' behind.

Don't go, I shout. Midway into the sky, Satan's daughter hears me and turns, diving down to the road where Phueth' is hissing at me and splaying his claws. She throws her wings over his body and enwraps him. With hand on her heart and a smile, she lets the harlot Lilith go, humming,

And I'll lead you all, wherever you may be. And I'll lead you all in the dance, said she.

Dance, say we!

Oh! Oh!........... O now I see.

Satan's daughter Liberty with Phueth' soar up into the sky, leaving me alone with Lilith.

Lilith and I now wish you all—wherever you may be—the Spirit of the Finis! Finis!

GORDON CHRISTENSON'S faith life ranged from Mormon to Episcopalian until his passing in March 2025. Law professor emeritus, law dean emeritus, lifetime elected fellow of the graduate school of the University of Cincinnati, father, brother, uncle, grandfather, and great-grandfather, Gordon's passion (as he said) was teaching students in jurisprudence, constitutional law, and international law. His many friends say he held a doctorate in the practice of friendship.

3

Further Along

ANDERSON COBB

Sometimes...I stop and take a look around. All around! On peaceful days...I watch the sunrise, hear the birds singing in the treetops, and look out into the wild blue yonder. It is then...I see beauty and magic...it is then, I see the wonder of life...and sometimes, I sing out loud!

I sing songs of joy, songs of love, and I sing those long-forgotten old Negro Spirituals. Songs...I heard sung by the church choir many years ago. A bit strange when I think about it today, but somehow when I was a growing up...this all seemed be laying a foundation for a better tomorrow. It was all there, and the preacher made it seem so easy. One needed only to keep faith, do good to mankind, and the Lord...would make a way somehow. I was a bit puzzled why throughout the history of mankind...there was so much toil and turmoil, so much hate, and so much war. Still, the very thought of it all...seemed grand. I imagined a life filled with beauty and happiness. And I still remember many of those old songs. The ease of the words flowing together gives me a feeling of joy today. So often, I recall the old deacons singing ...

Oh, when I come to the end of my journey
Weary of life, and the battle is won.

Carrying the staff, and the cross of redemption
He'll understand…and say, "Well done."

And I will rest at the close of the day.

I simply love those words. A great ending after overcoming a difficult task. Imagine a brave warrior, tattered, torn, and badly beaten claiming the reward. Those old songs are many. I love them still, and sometimes … sing them in the silence of my mind. But thinking back, the rhythm and harmony of the beautiful soprano voices of the women …mixing with the Bertones and Tenors of the male voices was truly angelic. And still, in the forefront of my mind is the time when the choir leader had me led off a verse of …"Peace in the Valley." It words are mesmerizing …

Well, the bear…will be gentle,
And the wolf…will be tame
And the lion shall lay down
by the lamb…oh yes.

It is a beautiful song, and it goes on to say …
The beasts from the wild
Shall be led by a child
And that I…me…I'll be changed…
changed…from the creature that I am…

Surely, all of us can point to times of struggle in our lives. For me, and in large part, I believe that it is the stormy night…that makes a sunny day so beautiful. All-in-all growing up my naiveite caused me think that faith alone would bring a better tomorrow. But such…was not the case.

And there are many who have traveled far rougher roads, endured more hardship, and many...who have not prevailed.

However, the years to follow would see me move further, away from the church; although, not necessarily away from the teachings of the Holy Bible. I struggled with seeing my mother, and her neighborhood friends barely scratch out a living. While people all around her filled with hate, prejudice and racism...lived in sheer luxury. They mocked her, they cursed her, and yet, they lived a life, the likes of which, she never dreamed of, a life...she never yearned for. And a life, she never had.

I wondered about the treatment of Black soldiers who fought in wars...to preserve our nation. I remember asking...why do Black people put so much faith in God? We as a people seemingly work harder, suffer more...and still have less. So...why is it, that our blessing comes only after a lifetime of struggle...and only after we die?

Well, as I grew older and learned about other religions in other nations, and practices in other civilizations. It was troubling that some practiced inflecting pain upon oneself, some even human sacrifices, and some reincarnation. The bottom line...was more and more of the same. The strong oppressing the weak, the rich, trampling over the poor, and all...hoping for a better tomorrow. I suppose, what troubled me most at that time was...how could it come to be that the people who enslaved our ancestors, mutilated and killed our men, beat, and raped our women ever become friends. And...why...would we want that to be?

In time I learned about the world at large...My eyes opened wide, and my spirits dampened even more when reading about slavery in Biblical times. Noted in the Book of Deuteronomy, a slave having worked for six years...was to be set free on the seventh year. For an instant I thought maybe the elders were right in saying...just be happy with what you have.

No matter the length of my questioning, it was usually met with... Son, we must keep our faith in God Almighty, there is nothing more we can do. I had much doubt, and was much younger then, so...I probably took too much at face value. Time would prove my hopes and dreams... to be just that. Hopes and dreams. My mother was fond of saying...keep your faith son...further along, we will get our blessing. And gentlemen... that brings me to the topic of my paper.

Further Along.
You see looking back! There were times...my mother would say, come along with me to church today. I want you to hear the preacher, preach the gospel, I want you hear the choir sing. Now, even though, she probably sensed that I was questioning my faith...she never let on, and I, never said. However, my mind was troubled by ever-present thoughts. I had many questions, questions that could not be answered by faith alone. Questions...that for me...challenged faith.

I thought of the many times, when I saw old Black men walking in the hot sun on a Sunday morning ...walking thru rain-soaked fields, pant legs rolled up, their shined shoes tied together flung over their shoulders, and their Sunday coats...hanging over their arms. My mother would say, we must do our best, to look our best...in the house of the Lord. And when I think about it, that house was little more than a two-room shack with a wood stove. And I wondered how life could be so hard for some, and so easy for others. Still, the words to an old spiritual trickled thru my mind. The beauty of the lyrics haunts my soul today.

Lord...sometimes I look up and wonder...what have I done, to make this race so hard to run. Then sayeth my soul...take courage...the Lord will make a way somehow!

You see, it sounded to me that the elders were in part, blaming themselves for the bitter times of life. Well, let me move on...I did learn a lot about life while attending those church services with my mother. There was one group of singers in particular, that she often spoke of. Many of her time...tried to capture their style. And to a degree, the purity in her voice sowed the seeds that grew around my heartstring. And even though those singers were long dead before I was born, their memory holds a place in my heart. Listening to recordings of their singing truly cemented my love of gospel music. In fact, learning of their struggles and perseverance somewhat renewed my waning faith.

All-in-all...as tough as it was for me growing up, it is almost unbelievable how hard life was for Black people in days just after emancipation. At any rate...this group of singers were truly remarkable, and their effect on me...is a story that must be told. To begin with, all but two of the group were former slaves, moreover, all of them battled prejudice, oppression, and worse. So, was it their faith, or relentless drive that helped them to sing their way into our nation's heart? They performed for Presidents...they performed for queens! And they toured the United States and Europe, singing songs that are now a cherished part of our country's musical heritage.

Today, we know and hear of Civil unrest, sometimes brutality, even at the hands of the law. I recall...a man gasping for life...left dying on the street. I recall a young woman in the comfort of her lover's arms being shot and killed in the middle of the night, and there are others. So... imperfection of law still looms in with us today. But life, for this group of young student singers was a whole different matter. Imagine...despite emancipation, and the fact that these freed slaves had been taught to read and write, the South was a very dangerous place for Black people in that day and time.

To a degree, there are people today who seemingly brush over the horrible acts of the Ku Klux Klan nightriders. But I ask you, and just for a moment...think of your sons...your daughters...being sat upon and assaulted, even horse-whipped by a ruthless gang. Well, that is exactly what routinely happened to some freed Blacks whose only crime was trying to teach other Blacks to read and write.

History tells the story of a member of this singing group being shot at in broad daylight while teaching in his classroom. Yet another young teacher had her school building burned to the ground. The sad fact is... nobody, nobody was ever punished for these horrific acts. I will not discuss the details in this writing, but there were times...many times when far...worse happened!

Think about it, back in 1871...barely 22 years before this very club was founded. A group of unknown Negro singers traveled far and wide hoping to make a difference. And keep in mind, some of them were just teenagers. They followed the path of the Underground Railway finally making their way here to Cincinnati. And as luck would have it, fortune swung their way when they sang before a national convention of influential ministers at Oberlin College...here in Ohio.

For the most part...they started with ballets common for the time. However, their leader was more moved by their singing of spirituals. So, after a ballet or two, they transitioned to songs like, *Steal Away, Swing Low Sweet Chariot*, and *This Little Light of Mine*. They also sang songs associated with slavery, and its dark past. These were songs sacred to elder African Americans, these were the songs my mother...loved. These were the songs that Black people secretly sang...only in the fields, and behind closed doors.

Well, their performance was a hit, but despite a warm reception, the collection plate totaled less than $50. Further, donations did not improve with repeat performances, and in the end collections barely covered expenses. Still, every singer stayed on with the group. Not a single one turned back.

Life on the road took its toll. And let me remind you, hotels and restaurants were generally closed to this group. Additionally, their leader, and many of the singers suffered from ills of the time, rheumatism, bronchitis, and chronic coughs. And resources being what they were...what clothes they had were literally worn to rags.

However, their triumphant performance in Oberlin gave a boost in bookings. And as word spread people were eager to hear them. Later, they appeared at Plymouth Church in Brooklyn New York, where they performed during a weekly prayer meeting held by Henry Ward Beecher, the first minister of Plymouth Church. And if you are wondering...he was the brother of Harriett Beecher-Stowe. Oddly enough, his church, like our club was formed in 1849. Moreover, it would become the foremost center of anti-slavery sentiment in the mid-19th century.

Perhaps, time heals all, but it would take nearly another 120 years before Plymouth Church would become a National Historic Landmark. At any rate, that performance was the spark that lit the fuse to this group's success. And from that time onward almost, every church wanted to hear this singing group of. They performed for Mark Twain, and even, President Ulysses S. Grant, congressmen, and other diplomats.

Now...talk about perseverance, with less than two weeks' rest, they were back on the road, touring the Eastern Part of the United States. In time, they toured Europe to universal acclaim and sang for the royal families of Holland, Germany, and Britain. But here again, the road was rough, really rough. And even though the group raised what today would be millions of dollars, but they were paid a pittance.

The relentless schedule worn all of them down. On top of that, their advance scout suffered a nervous breakdown. And the group's leader wife died of typhoid fever, and he himself nearly died of a pulmonary hemorrhage. As I said earlier, life was hard. Not only did they face discrimination on the road, the press, was far from favorable. Add to that sickness, namely tuberculosis and you can imagine the impact it had on the singers.

Then came a grueling tour of Germany...ninety-eight days, thru forty-one towns, sixty-eight concerts. This in turn contributed to low morale, frayed nerves, and some rivalry. And after nearly seven years of touring, they returned home. However, and looking back a bit here, despite having to overcome strong opposition...that trip to Oberlin Ohio to perform was a turning point for the group. Imagine their delight, if you will...former slaves, that now could read and write, count their money, and choose their own names.

Their leader...George Leonard White was a kind man. In hard times, he used his own savings to help keep things afloat. But did you know... he was also the treasure, and music professor for the school. A school so desperate to raise money; that in a daring fundraising effort, he proposed forming a singing group of the most gifted students and taking them on a fundraising tour of the North.

Their start had little support, even before they left town, they encountered strong resistance. Some parents were afraid for their children. Additionally, fellow teachers opposed the tour, and the American Missionary Association, the very organization that operated the school...refused to help. Their concern was the singing group's appeal for money... might jeopardize their own fundraising activities.

At any rate this group of nine members ...five women and four men sat out on a national tour not knowing what their outcome would be. Still, their strength and endurance enabled them to withstand incredible hardship and struggle. And to my way of thinking...faith intervened amidst heart and mind in times of trouble. And I'd like to think inspired by Biblical reference and guided by a message in the Book of Leviticus speaking of the "Year of Jubilee!" A year...in which all enslaved people would be set free. At any rate the singing group took a new name...and are forever known as...**"The Jubilee Singers."**

In the end...the group my mother so often talked about. A singing group that changed my life so completely...is one of the earliest, and most-famous vocal groups in "Black History". You see...back in 1871 this group of African American singers came about in a university established in an effort to educate formerly enslaved Black people. This school was originally known as the Fisk Free Colored School. So, there you have it... Fisk University of Nashville, Tennessee.

Now, I cannot, and I do not proclaim to have either suffered, or endured anything akin to the experiences of "The Jubilee Singers." No, my question is...how, could anyone stay so true to a cause...how could anyone keep faith in a promise that nobody has ever witnessed coming to be? How could anyone...keep waiting for tomorrow after so long a time, after so much hardship, and after so much pain.

My experiences over the years have taught me a few things. Top of which...life, is not fair...business, is not fair! But I...see life itself, as an unimaginable miracle. From the tiniest microbe...to the fish that swim the sea, from the nuisance of the gnat...to the ferocity of the lion, life to me appears not to be happenstance. And although for my family and kind...life, has all but passed us by. Still, my belief is...that there must be something more!

I think back to The Jubilee Singers performing what were once called...slave songs. Songs...that today, we proudly call African American Spirituals. So, sometimes on a peaceful day...I take a look around, admire the beauty of the sunrise, hear birds singing in the treetops. Sometimes...I look out into the wild blue yonder and see the beauty, and magic I saw as a child. I relive dreams of yesteryear, and think whether my tomorrow be mind and body, or mind and spirit...I am moved to faith and sometimes sing out loud!

So!

Further along...I will put aside my playthings, soar high alongside the eagle, look down over arid lands, and sail out across the sea.

Further along...I will dawn my Sunday best, step off the streetcar, never awaiting the sunrise to dry the morning dew

Further along...I will build a house high on the hill by the running waters, till land of my own...and in the evening, I will rest...alongside of an old dog.

A long time ago...prejudice joined hands with racism, marred the tablet on which I had laid my plans, and hatred, blocked almost every door.

A long time ago...the streetcar...the bus...and the train, even when almost empty, had few seats. And jobs in office buildings...were but shadows of promises be.

A long time ago...my father died ten years before I was seventeen. Still, I remember only the kind words spoken of him.

A long time ago...I wandered without certainty, without pause, and without measuring the strides that could lead one astray.

A long time ago...I held my mother's hand, felt a measure of truth, and learned the value of staying the course.

Even now...the man in the mirror looking back at me...is very different from whom I had always longed to be.

Even now...sometimes I wonder if I have set my sights too high, if I have taken the right path, and...and why some think me...a lesser man.

Just a while ago...I sat looking out of the window at the falling rain, memories nourishing thoughts of times gone by.

Perhaps somewhere...angels dwell, perhaps a Heaven...perhaps, a Hell

But until the doors to opportunity and freedom...are opened wide

The promise of salvation, and a better tomorrow...is left behind.

So, Further along...I will keep wandering...I will keep waiting, hoping that time...will mend the parts, that are broken.

ANDERSON COBB is man of many thoughts and ideas about life and thereafter. Proud son of a sharecropper, educated in the Jim Crowe South before coming to Cincinnati, Ohio; where he attended the Al Gable Art School and was formally trained in Commercial Art.Later in life helearned photography and A/V multimedia. He is the photographer of the Cincinnati Tri-Centennial Time Capsule to be opened in 2088. Now retired, he enjoys life as a poet and painter.

4

A MASHUGGA CHRISTMAS

LEE COMER

It was late December just a few days before Christmas. It had snowed the night before, making everything shimmer and glisten a sparkly and iridescent white in the late morning sun. The landscape made it seem more like we lived in an upper class, well-to-do part of town, but in fact we really lived in a middle-class neighborhood. Well, maybe it was more lower-middle-class—in a middle-class house, which could desperately have used a fresh coat of paint. Our town itself was a thriving midwestern industrial community—in the rust belt actually.

My sister Carol and I were out playing in the snow that morning. Rather than making snow angels, snowballs or snow people out of the freshly fallen snow, we were jabbering incessantly about Christmas and what we would get, or not get, from Santa this year.

We were maybe four or five at the time. We weren't really poor, but we weren't really rich either, maybe somewhere in between. We had already visited Schoenberg's Department Store to sit on Santa's lap, confide in him and get a whiff of something strangely harsh on his breath. And we had each written our letters to Santa. It took us quite a while before we finally figured out why our mother would always "mail them" for us, rather than each of us just taking them down to the mailbox ourselves.

We had a rule in our family. We could each wish for three things from Santa, and we were absolutely guaranteed to get one of them. I had written down a bow and arrow, a slingshot and a bb gun. My sister had written down a doll house, a doll house and a doll house. I think I should add that she later became an intellectual property attorney.

We were only out there a while before we heard the familiar cry. "Hey, you guys!" came a boisterous shout, a line which opened a popular kids show back in the day. A few of us who were in the know used it as a sort of "top secret" greeting throughout the neighborhood. Beckoning us were Ben and Rosie from next door, our best friends and playmates who were about our age. They had come out to play, too. We hadn't seen one another for a while, based on the differences in each of our schools' Christmas vacation schedules. They didn't get off for Christmas vacation like we did. We couldn't understand that at the time. But we couldn't wait to talk to them about Christmas and ask them what they might be getting from Santa.

"We don't have Christmas," said Benny. "We're Jewish. I thought you knew that. We have Hanukah instead."

We both knew they were Jewish, although we didn't exactly know what that meant. All we knew was that the family owned the carry-out and deli down the street and we would get an occasional free soda or Clark bar when we went down there with them. That apparently was something that made them Jewish and we liked that.

"No Christmas!" we exclaimed. "No Santa? No presents? No Christmas tree?" We couldn't get over it. It was the first we had heard of such a thing. "No way," we said.

"C'mon. We'll show you," Benny said. He and Rosie led us over, across the driveway and the slowly melting snow, to their house.

When we got there, smack in the middle of their front door hung about the largest holly wreath we had ever seen. "That's our Hanukah wreath," they said.

Inside their house was all lit up like a, well, you-know-what. Christmas lights, candles, big red bows and decorations were everywhere. "These are our Hanukah lights and decorations," Rosie and Benny said, pointing all around, and directing our attention to the many little items and displays of their holiday decor.

"And what's really great about it," both Rosie and Ben explained, "is that it lasts for eight straight days."

"Each day we get another present Another Hanukah present. For eight straight days," Benny added.

At that point we noticed the huge—and I mean huge—Christmas tree in the corner of the room, covered with lights and ornaments, top to bottom. It was like nothing we had ever seen before. "That's our Hanukah tree," said Rosie. "It's great, don't you think?"

And underneath it sat a bicycle, a doll buggy, an electric train, roller skates and a number of other toys. "Those are our Hanukah gifts. And we've still got a few more days of Hanukah to go. We can't wait."

"Where did all those presents and toys come from that are under the tree?" we asked. "How did they get there?"

Rosie and Ben pointed over to the fireplace on the other side of the room. "You see," they explained, "every day, for eight straight days, Father

Hanukah comes down the chimney, late at night, bringing each of us a new toy or gift. And he places it under the tree."

It was at that point that we heard the distant call. "Carol, Bobby, it's lunch time." Distant though it was, we could hear it loud and clear. "It's Mom," we said. "We gotta go."

We hurried down the stairs, back across the driveway and the newly trodden snow, and in our back door like in a flash. There was our Mom in the kitchen covering slices of a newly opened loaf of Wonder Bread with thick, sweet, gooey sandwich makings.

"Mom, we want to be Jewish," I shouted. "We want to be Jewish," Carol loudly repeated. We couldn't have emphasized it more.

Our Mom didn't even look up. She just continued spreading. "Go tell your little buddies you can be Jewish if you want but I'm not going to be making your peanut butter and jelly sandwiches on matzo."

LEE COMER is a student of days gone by—a time of easier living, less stress, greater tolerance, and a greater ability to laugh at ourselves and the many differences between us. Lee has written extensively on these days in award-winning screenplays and teleplays. As a career advertising copywriter, he was ultimately elected president of his agency, Packo Mitchell Hanson & Comer. But he still had to write copy all day and every day.

Feast of The Pronunciation

Angels gather in their
nimbus around what is most delicious to say:
around *sycamore* they float
like cottonwood drift or ash of burnt roses.
Great applause breaks out
after *marmoreal* presents itself, fluted, columnar,
casting light like milky rhinestones
in a mirror.

And then your name, love, enters the room
and the day falls to its knees
and even the passing moments soften
into gold and flow before you
like a vanguard of honey,

holy, nearly
unspeakable.

– RICHARD HAGUE

5

PHILOSOPHY 101

JOSEPH J. DEHNER

Shakespeare scripted Antonio to proclaim in *The Tempest*, "What's past is prologue." Withrow High School was my prologue to college. Our senior class of 830 was diverse and integrated, as Cincinnati public schools were before parents fled with their baby boom kids to one-acre lots that gobbled up farmland outside the district's boundaries. Offspring of wealthy families attended costly private schools or a public school in a private town of 3-to-5 acre lots called Indian Hill.

My Dad and I drove to New Jersey over the tunnel-studded Pennsylvania Turnpike in August 1966. Princeton granted me sophomore status, thanks to ample Advanced Placement courses offered then at Withrow. But the alumni schools committee interviewer warned with a knowing grin, "You'll meet a lot of people a lot smarter than you." He didn't mention class or money, but I suppose that was implied.

I prepared by reading *This Side of Paradise*, a Fitzgerald primer about how a middle-class kid from land between the coasts who didn't attend boarding school might compete and congeal with the American aristocracy of lineal descendant wealth. I bought a faded madras sports jacket at Goodwill that I thought might emit a whiff of old money, as though a costume could work as a blending agent. To my surprise, my brethren (Princeton went coed in my senior year) were a far more diverse bunch than I'd assumed.

Philosophy 101 was a mandatory class I couldn't avoid by arriving as a sophomore. Professor Carl Gustav Hempel taught us or tried to. His thick German accent stifled easy receipt of profound wisdom hurled from a lectern toward an upward slanting bowl of wooden seats and curled writing surfaces with initials carved into them by long-graduated mis-

creants. A guy next to me whispered as he entered the gothic hall for the first lecture, "We read his epistemology at Exeter." Withrow's curriculum did not feature Hempel or inform me what an epistemologist does for a living. I made a funnel in industrial arts class. My creation leaked, but it went to my Dad as a Christmas offering anyway. He must have cringed inside while complimenting me on the poorly soldered device.

Classmates I assumed went to prep school seemed riveted by the oration from the stage. Hempel recited without notes as fluidly as water over Niagara. He had the habit of propping his oversized, rather square head onto both forearms while holding forth. His brain must be heavier than mine, I drifted. Up float ed an image of the backyard frog statue in my mother's rock garden - an amphibian version of Rodin's The Thinker. At least I knew how to pronounce Rodin, I reassured myself. But the furious notes taken by my Exeter classmate indicated that I might not be following the lessons that must be flowing to others like honey from the stage. And what if I missed a point that would show up on the exam?

In those days, first semester spelled doom for a few who couldn't make the intellectual cut. Along with a General Motors scholarship that covered tuition and my parents' support, I worked the dining halls, so paying for the experience was handled. Most first-year courses I thought wouldn't fail me or me them. But Philosophy 101 - the very title seemed to demand an Everest climb of thought. Would I plunge into a crevice? When Hempel uttered that logical empiricism was an articulation of the deductive-nomological model of scientific explanation, my brain either tuned out or rebelled, I don't recall which, as though it was fending off an alien attack like the one Orson Welles set in New Jersey for his Halloween 1938 "War of the Worlds" radio broadcast. Off romped Hempel in a rapturous journey of polysyllabic utterances. I felt a stranger in a strange land, though I'd enjoyed Heinlen's novel by that title the summer before arriving in New Jersey's midlands.

"I do not give examinations," said Hempel toward the end of the course. "A paper—write an exposition on a topic of your choice. Select a proposition you wish to prove, then prove it." My prep school classmate didn't make a note about that, appearing to expect the assignment as though he'd been trained for such a test. Perhaps he had a notebook of papers ready to reuse or adapt. "Write a paper" was not how Withrow tested.

Seventeen can be a dividing line for guys. Some go to prison from a moment's mistake. Some die in car crashes. Some get girls pregnant. Some enter the Army, but Vietnam made enlistment not the attraction it was in the late 50's and early 60's, when a trip to Korea or Germany sounded like adventure instead of a death sentence. The last half of the 1960's sharpened our awareness of self-preservation. That's it, I decided, I will write a paper about that—not Vietnam, but why we choose what we do. "Selfishness"—this must be life's meta-meta theory. I will set out to prove that all we do we do from selfishness. We act universally to preserve ourselves and maximize our self-interest. My paper would set out to prove this. It seemed self-evident and eminently sensible. Proof would merely be a matter of writing convincingly, no research needed, just well-phrased words in literately constructed sentences.

The result was the worst grade I ever received in anything. Looking back 58 years later, I can grasp that Hempel treated my opus with mercy rather than total condemnation. Today I ponder it as one of the best lessons I ever got from a teacher. When people say we learn more from our failures than from our victories, my selfishness paper could serve as trial exhibit A.

If everything is selfish, Hempel wrote in red on my opus, then you have said nothing — anything that is everything fails to have meaning. After the shock of a grade that was like a C-minus or D-plus on a high school grading scale, I comforted myself that at least I didn't flunk. And the lesson struck its target. Words are how we distinguish one thing from another. "Selfish" has meaning if it describes a difference from what is unselfish or different from the motivation or reason behind other acts. To say that "selfishness" describes everything we do deprives the message of any substance. I'd written a paper that disproved the very point I was aiming to prove - and yet had turned it in.

We submitted our papers before Hempel's last lecture. I listened attentively to this one, having become accustomed to piercing through his accent to the meaning of his discourse. His final comments were about a one-syllable word.

"What is mud?" he asked, propping his head upon his knuckles on the lectern, waiting for the question to resonate within our skulls. "If there is anything you have learned from our time together, I hope it is this."

I edged forward, focused like a laser, unwilling to lose a syllable to Germanic intonation.

"Mud is not ground with water added."

I could get that.

"And mud is not water with earth mixed into it."

He paused, like Groucho Marx ready to spring a punch line. Revelation was about to grace the hall.

"Mud is mud."

With that, Professor Hempel turned and plodded to the door. My Exeter classmate leapt to his feet. Thunderous applause flooded the hall. Classmates pounded on their desktops.

Mud is mud.

JOE DEHNER drove a Volkswagen through the Soviet Union in 1969 before settling on an international law career. Words matter to attorneys, and especially to clients. A past president of The Literary Club, Joe set out to shed legalese and craft fiction, with a novel (*The Seventh Trumpet*) and numerous short stories published (see josephdehner.com). He and beloved Noël, two daughters, and three grandgirls reside in Cincinnati.

6

Showing Her
A Good Time

RICHARD HAGUE

At the end of my senior year of high school, I boycotted prom. My buddy and I slouched and smirked at the entrance of the dance, wearing scruffy t-shirts and jeans and those crooked, wise-guy leers that my friend John Ray confirms were characteristic of so many upper Ohio River boys. Exactly what we were protesting, I cannot recall. Phony pomp and circumstance? Fake pretty? That expensive commercial rip-off ritual? Or was it just aimless adolescent orneriness on our parts?

The dance was being held in St. John Arena, a structure erected by the Diocese of Steubenville behind my alma mater, Catholic Central High School. It was a hard brutalist building with a cruelly slick concrete floor on which an obese track coach, it was said, once broke his leg trying to show boys how to jump hurdles. Our high school Phys. Ed. classes were held there. Prom night, that pig of a building was lipsticked with a few blue and gold bows and balloons, the school colors of the CCHS Crusaders. My friend and accomplice Johnny Sellaroli and I watched the couples promenade in dresses bright and magnificent, the boys' tuxedos sometime blaringly over the top in terms of style and color—along the lines of what was known around those times and in that place as "the full Cleveland." Despite the clothes misadventures, those boys knew better than I did how to show a girl a good time; after the dance they would go to restaurants like The Green Lantern, or to the Country Club, if their families belonged, or to the famous roadhouse on the way to Pittsburgh whose name I have forgotten. Warm memories would be made that night. My protest of the event might have damaged me in some way; showing a girl a good time in traditional terms—wining and dining, fancy clothes, romantic evenings in romantic places—never my strength, certainly even less so after that. Maybe our incapacity for natural social smoothness was the underlying reason for our dismissal of it all. Later, a fully grown man, I even failed at normal marriage protocol: after a patient wait of a couple of years, my girlfriend, the dear woman, proposed to me on Sadie Hawkins Day, in a Cincinnati pizza joint. At the time, this did not seem problematic to me.

Besides, under even the best of circumstances, a legal good time in Steubenville in those days was hard to find. After the Friday dances and the Saturday night football games, about the most exciting thing was to get pizza at DiCarlo's, a family operation that employed silent Dean Martin doppelgangers in white t-shirts who stood before hot ovens, now and again pulling pans out of one and shoving them into another, steam rising, and then slamming them down on the counter, flicking out rounds of pepperoni like Vegas dealers, then slicing the whole pan into the squares we bought for ten cents a piece. Eating three or four with your girlfriend was considered by most "showing her a good time." So I didn't have a lot of practice in the finer points of showing a girl a good time, nor did the reverse pizza-parlor proposal years later demonstrate much progress in my understanding of what made such a thing

Nearly four decades later, my wife (the very saintling who had proposed to me so long ago) and I were staying at a B & B in Harmar Village, a historic settlement just across the mouth of the Muskingum River from the oldest town in Ohio. The place was called The House on

Harmar Hill. From its front porch you could see downtown Marietta, where the riverfront Lafayette Hotel is named after the Revolutionary War general.

We had enjoyed walking around old Harmar Village, and I had been showing my wife what I thought was a pretty decent time. The occasion was our 40th wedding anniversary, and I had paid special attention to making sure we had a nice place to stay and a relaxing weekend of vacationing in a scenic Appalachian region outside of our long residence in Cincinnati. We had by then eaten at a couple of nice places in town, which I knew pretty well after decades of ridge-running and creek paddling in southeastern Ohio. In fact, I owned a camp less than thirty miles north, in Monroe County. Marietta is the seat of Washington County, having been settled by a band of New England revolutionaries who organized themselves into the Ohio Company at The Bunch of Grapes Tavern in Cambridge, MA. Interred in its cemetery lie more of Washington's officers than in any other in the country. Little historical tidbits like this, I imagined, would up the good time chances with Pam.

Offhandedly, I said to her, "Let's drive up to The Woods," which is what I called my camp at the time, earlier known by my father as "The Farm" or "The Ponderosa. "It's less than an hour. We can just drive by and see how things are."

The Woods were not Pam's favorite destination. I think the only time she had been there before was around the time of our courting. We'd driven over from Cincinnati during the Easter break; I remember she wore a green flannel shirt, and that we slept through a chilly night, fully clothed, in the back of my pickup truck. (Do you see what I mean about muffing a good time?) After I foolishly mentioned the snakes, which had to be collected from the kitchen drawers and the closets of the trailer at the beginning of each spring visit, she vowed never to set foot in the tiny Airstream-wanna-be my dad had hauled down there a few years before.

By the time of our drive up from Marietta, there was a new trailer. Not actually new, but new to my dad and me. It was almost as old as I was, having been built in 1949, so when we visited that day, it was probably in its early sixties.

My dad's and then later my own rustications to The Woods broke a lot of Mrs. Hague's household rules—I mean those promulgated by my mother, that Mrs. Hague. Even more dismissive than Pam, early in the saga of the place my mom had written it off as a godforsaken hovel in the sticks, worthy only of trailer trash (of which tribe I am proud to claim my father and I promptly became honorary members after our first stay). Besides, it was a hopeless money sink and would probably be contributory, in the long run, to my father's demise. Before he died, she'd tried to talk him out of leaving it to me for fear I'd be burdened with its costs of upkeep.

Years before, my dad and I had come down to The Woods to find the original trailer laying on its side, blown over by some mammoth gust, the cable anchoring it broken and coiled beside it on the ground. That wind must have been something like what wrecked the airship Shenandoah not far away in Noble County in 1925. You can still visit the crash site, and there's a museum-in-a-trailer containing relics and memorabilia. The nearby Noble-Shenandoah high school teams are called the Zeps. Pieces of the wreckage sold recently on the Internet for several hundred dollars.

I speak of these various ruinations because that's what Pam and I found when we pulled up the grassy path and stepped up onto the porch of the "new" trailer that day. Something or someone had shattered both the big picture windows, roughly three by four feet each, near the head of the trailer. The glass was entirely crazed; could I detect a bullet hole? Whatever had happened—an earthquake brought on by fracking which was becoming widespread in the county, a deliberate or accidental deer-hunter's slug, some poor, opioid-crazed locals desperate for anything to rip off for sale, or a violent gale twisting the whole trailer enough to stress the glass—the windows were ruined. I looked at Pam and said, "We can't leave it like this. We're going to have to fix them."

There were a few problems with this impromptu plan. One, I didn't have the keys to the padlock of the trailer. We hadn't planned on being near The Woods when we left on what was soon to fall from the name of "vacation" to something more like "ordeal." There was no direct way in. Two, I had no tools with me; in the trailer were the minimum basics: claw hammer, screwdriver, pliers. Three, the closest place to even begin some sort of temporary repair was in Woodsfield, the county seat twelve miles away, where the hardware store dispensed not only tools and paint but also, thank God, lumber.

Pam got into the car with me. The way to Woodsfield from the trailer, on Greebrier Ridge outside the village of Graysville, is as windy a way as you can find in Ohio; more than once during my rustications there I narrowly escaped death in head-ons with teenage neighbors speeding up and around one of a dozen blind bends.

At the hardware store, a trim, tanned gentleman in a gray plaid flannel shirt asked if he could help. After I delivered an abbreviated narration of the beginning of this tale (things aren't rushed in Monroe County; some sort of small talk is appropriate at the beginning of any transaction), he fetched us a sheet of plywood and cut it into a pair of four-by four panels that would fit in the back of Pam's station wagon. Then off we rode, back to The Woods.

The repair was difficult. I had to break out all the remaining window glass; most of it fell down between the trailer and the porch, where it lay out of easy reach.

Pam was patiently attentive so far; no eye-rolling or huffing. After breaking out the glass and briefly imagining the prospect of my severing a femoral artery on some jagged shard, I clambered inside and looked around. No damage. But this was mid-June, with mild weather and no direct way in through the shattered windows yet. Now I had somehow to fasten the plywood over the openings. One side was easy: some ten-penny nails and the first sheet was fast and tight. But how was I, from the outside, going to get the other fastened securely? I remembered an old trick and drove a nail through the middle of the plywood, wiggled it around to enlarge the hole, and ran a nail with a piece of string tied to what would be the interior end. Then levering the plywood up the inside, I lowered one leg at a time out onto the porch and pulled on the string to lift the plywood firmly in position. Then I pounded nails into the window frame around to wedge it into and pulled it tight. I was at no point convinced that this arrangement would withstand the gusts of the first thunderstorm, but it was all I could do.

I put the hammer in the back of Pam's car. By now, this was half an entire day after we'd arrived on our ostensibly brief drive-by just to see how things were. I took one last look at the situation—the jury-rigged plywood window covers, the remnants of glass all over, the fading of the eight-year-old paint job on the trailer, the punky deterioration of the wooden porch itself. Pam sidled squarely into my sight, and said, with a kind of Charlie Brown grin, "Hague, you really know how to show a girl a good time."

What I still didn't know at the time, but unforgettably know now, is that this would be one of her truest, most piercing lines in all our marriage. And it was an obvious no-brainer of an observation that I had somehow failed to really internalize for more than six decades of my male existence. It was Knowledge in the form of a hammer. Knowledge like a small explosion. A gob-smack of Truth.

Startled, knowing immediately how right she was in her (loving) sarcasm, I think I even coughed up a hic of a laugh. A bitter little one, yes indeed: bitter...and literally unmanning.

RICHARD HAGUE is author or editor of 23 collections of prose and poetry. He is winner of the 1985 CoPoet of the Year from the Ohio Poetry Association for *Ripening* (The Ohio State University Press 1984), 2003 Appalachian Poetry Book of the Year for *Alive in Hard Country* (Bottom Dog Press), and the 2012 Weatherford Award in Poetry for *During The Recent Extinctions: New & Selected Poems* 1984-2012 (Dos Madres Press).

7

the right word: grist

R I C H A R D   H U N T

Here's an impossible ask: query your friendly neighborhood author to ante up *the right word*. Don't expect much in response, aside from obfuscation, indignation and rebuttal. To show how challenging this quandary might be, imagine being the server at some fancy-pants restaurant and asking a table of diners about their meal, with their reply being, "mmmm, it's indignant." Not the right word, clearly. But let's muck around a bit before trying again.

Referencing Eliz. Barrett Browning's *Sonnet #43*, most folks know its opening line "Let me count the ways. I love thee to the depth and breadth and height." But with this vexing *the right word* prompt, you only get to pick one. Should it be depth? Or breadth? Or height?

It is fair to ask, Why just one right word? How about two or twenty-two? Is it even possible that there can be just one? To pick "the right word" is like asking "Who's the greatest running back of all-time?"* While the pigskin game still has the same name, almost every other aspect -- the equipment, the plays, even the cities and teams -- has changed over the decades. * In this instance, there is a single answer: Jim Brown. Granted, he's no one's first draft pick as a life coach,

but even Hollywood special effects failed when trying to tackle him. Uh-oh, is my Cleveland showing?

Finding the right word is akin to coaxing a quiver of *le mot juste* cobras to rise from their wicker baskets, then correctly picking out which one is going to strike first. Don't look them in the eye, that truly annoys them. The good news is that cobra venom takes half an hour to "work" so as long as you have your snakebite kit handy, no pressure. But if you forgot to stash that handy-dandy lifesaver in your go-bag, there is a right word in this instance, and it's HELP!

The Sisyphean challenge to find the Swiss-knife, one-size-fits-all, everything word is nearly, but not clearly, pointless. The OED includes over 170,000 English language words that are supposedly in use, although most folks scrape by with ~10% of that total. Still and all, with a million words having at one time been written, typed or etched, then read silently or aloud while possibly illuminated by torchlight all the way up through tungsten, you'd think by now we'd happen upon at least one perfect word. Maybe one we also liked the sound when spoken. Or a word that's as pleasurable to look at as it is to recite, like an e.e. cummings's poem.

AI as the modern-day Oracle of Delphi, would gladly proffer a term, or two, or three. Go ahead and pluck one. You won't get any specificity from a program that's akin to WordCloud on speed. Don't like that one, how about this one? Don't-like-that-one-how-about-this-one?

Don'tlikethatonehowaboutthisone?

Don'tlikethatonehowaboutthisone?

DON'TLIKETHATONEHOWABOUTTHISONE?

To cut to the quick: Literarians know that there's really no one-word-fits-all in terms of right, tight, and terse in verse. It's mind-blowing impossible to calculate all the plausible sentences that the tumbling words-dice in the Yahtzee cup can render: an essay, a story, an epic poem, or daily journal passage. Or an email never read before being deleted, a text rant you will regret immediately after sending, a non-rant but instead a thank you note. As a quick aside, Yahtzee admittedly is a unique word but extremely limited to game-playing. Definitely not prime material for stand-up comedy. Patient: "Doc, I've got a Yahtzee right here in my gut. Can't sleep. Can't take a deep breath. Do you think I'm going to die?" Answer: "Yes, but hopefully not before you leave my office." Spelunking, sure, also fun to say, but likewise limited versatility and a major phobia for most folks. Like the steed in "The Wizard of Oz," *the right word* can be the horse of many colors.

There's long been a Greek chorus of literary legends advising authors to navigate the thesauri of their vocabularies carefully. Mark Twain's river-song accent advises authors to avoid the $5 word when a fifty-cent coin will do. More from Mr. Clemens later. Bear in mind, though, his counsel to beware the bright and shiny object is smart. Fledgling word-birds flutter their new feathers peacock-like, but they seldom fly.

Personally, my unfortunate fascination with and misapplication of exotic words would inevitably bloom like red wine spilled on a white tablecloth: tsunami was employed to convey feeling overwhelmed, but sadly I flaunted it about without grasping the tragic human loss usually tied to the word; woebegone should have indeed been-gone; and perhaps the more egregious faux pas (and I can feel the heat rise in my cheeks with this memory since shame is the only emotion that's felt with the same intensity in recollection as was wrought at the first instance), was my long-ago use of the word pimp as a synonym for acne, directed at my little sister while at the dinner table. If you'd like to identify the poster boy for painful misuse and abuse of the dictionary without reading the warning labels ...that's me in the post office Wanted gallery.

Hence we find ourselves at a crossroads. The East-West route follows the "there-is-no-single-right-word" (East) to "any-word-will-do-as-long-as-its-grammatically-correct" (West) coordinates. Here is indeed a second railing against AI: if an author really doesn't care how something is said, then party on, Garth, sign your name to whatever mess you get back. Ask the digital temptress to provide 2500 words on Subject X and you'll get something that's possibly correct but definitely unremarkable. Moreso, it could be the same output that countless other folks might receive if using the same instructions. It's true that these E-W directionals allow writers to increase their production, plus it's less work, but pablum is pablum, nonetheless. To invoke the oft-used example of an infinite number of chimpanzees at an infinite number of typewriters yielding the collected works of Shakespeare, what AI provides the unwitting is an infinite number of writers typing at an infinite number of computers—complete with high-speed broadband—all coming up with the same "All work and no play makes Jack a dull boy" right before things get really dark (thanks to Stephen King's "The Shining" for such a wonderfully gruesome reference).

Whereas a North-South sojourn fittingly aspires along the spines of mountain ridges, i.e., a route where hard work and potential reward reach beyond any previous summits. Grab pitons, crampons, and pick-axes; authorial steps forward need to be anchored by *the right word(s)* chiseled into sentences. Such a quest is not for the faint of heart as it's thin air when scaling new writing heights. Similarly, it's true that gemstones and precious metals are usually mined in mountainous areas (this is not nature's way to make them hard to find, it's just the scientific process; to make mountains massive tectonic plates are forced against, and ultimately atop, one another, generating heat and pressure which then sprinkles the bright and shiny treasures within)—so aspiring, perspiring and stertorous authors should look for these jewels as they move upward, word by word.

As I've been pushing words around for 45 years (aka publishing, be it books, journals, newspapers and/or magazines), the harsh reality is that there are two overriding factors in any and all ongoing/eternal biblio battles. The wise writer will always look to 1. Connect with readers with words that entice, educate, enlighten and entertain, and 2. Follow the editorial guidelines of the organization in charge, i.e. they who pay the bills. Only after those two sacrosanct edicts come the opportunity to pursue *the right word(s)*.

Truly, unless you masochistically choose to self-edit, self-publish, self-finance, self-distribute, and self-collect, you should endeavor to use words that the readership relishes in a format which the printer/publisher approves. Very little in publishing, or life, comes free. In the case of gratis advice, oft-times you get what you pay for. On the other hand, beware of any soothsayers promising a purchased spot on the bestseller list. The number one best book promotion remains word-of-mouth, which means lots of folks have to read the book, have to like the book, and have to tell all their friends about it ...at work, at the bar, and/or online.

A goodly number of years ago, USIA publishing-bookselling cultural exchanges with former Soviet-bloc countries shuttled five well-intentioned panelists for week-long visits to US embassies and cultural centers in Romania, Hungary, and Russia, with directives to deliver two three-hour long presentations per day. Half of the audience thought we were spies (the preceding agency was the USIS which was notoriously rife with covert operatives). It's not hard to understand our hosts' suspicions because for non-English speakers, USIA and USIS look almost identical, because the former is unpronounceable, and the latter sounds like "useless". At the conclusion of our week in Bucharest, one of the attendees gifted each of us one of his books. For context, at that time the cost of a book in their new free-market economy equaled a month's wages. This meant that this young man just gave our group the ungodly equivalent of five month's rent, food, and utilities. All five of us tried to thank him for this monumental generosity while at the same time putting the book(s) back in his hands, imploring that he sell them to make some leu and bani. As a coda, not one of us could read Romanian, so this indecipherable volume could have been filled with a plethora of "right words" but for us, would have simply been an extra two pounds in the backpack all the way home. "Please, your gift is very kind, but please share it with a countryman here at the conference." There were no *right words* on either side of the dialogue in this instance.

* * * *

Recovering from some surgery was virtually an annual event for me from 1980-1999. To prepare for the post-procedure hours of inactivity, I piled up books to ward off the narcoleptic effects of anesthesia while also serving as distraction from whatever appendage was swathed in ace bandages and Mad Max armature. In 2018, hoping for honorable acclamation by accepting a knee replacement (ultimately a conditional surrender), I aimed higher: Robert Penn Warren's *All the King's Men*. I was so slack-jawed enthralled with his mastery that I reminded myself to not simply scan each page's final line in a reader's haste to thumb, pinch and turn to the next page. I may be projecting, but my take on poets' narratives (and Penn Warren self-described his life as "started as a poet and will probably end as a poet") is that they seem to pay more attention to the nuance of individual words. Similarly, the works of Jarrell, Malouf, Plath, Lerner, Angelou, Ondaajte et. al. confirm this supposition. Truly, it's no surprise that poets as wordsmiths tend to be connoisseurs of *le mot juste*.

A more pertinent piece of advice from Mark Twain is when he wrote "The difference between the *almost right* word and the *right* word is really a large matter. 'Tis the difference between the lightning bug and the lightning." To walk that lesser path, to be the more meandering flaneur, risks writing with an eye first on high style/low effort instead of dovetailing chiseled words preceding the nouns and verbs that do the heavy lifting. To find the perfect fit and fix in the composition's joinery is a Job #1 with succinctity [sic], or perhaps *sic-cinctity* *[sic-sick]* in this case.

As writers, the first task is to be stenographer for the audio-ticker tape in our heads, to let the words flow unimpeded and without judgment. Double-checking for *right words* comes with revision, but then we must turn off that soundtrack so we can re-read, recite aloud, and revise what was furiously scrawled. Because ultimately, what we write must be understandable. To have fun on the page, well fine, if that's how you warm up, sure, but afterwards, let the red pen run free.

When we think of the all-stars, so many of the must-reads leaned on words that echoed their persona: Robert Frost, Rachel Carson, and Papa Hemingway found flinty, sharp, strong, hard, punchy, earthy terms. Whereas others—Wilde, Proust, Woolf—wound words into flowery phrases to evoke a luxurious, languorous, sensitivity to life's eddies and currents.

But to come full circle, we must agree that there is no universal right word. Wink-wink, secret handshake. With that behind us, could it, would it, might it be possible to choose a favorite word just for the fun of it? Like finding your spirit animal. It doesn't need to be a word that works in every situation, but if there's a gap that calls for something special, let's turn it loose. Think of this as the Literary Club's version of Wordle meets Rock/Paper/Scissors, topped with a little Scrabble.

Believing that those who throw down the glove need to first find their second (I so wanted to use those last four words as a phrase for so long, and for what it's worth, my second will either Webster or Roget as their age infers that they also had musket experience) then to run the gauntlet myself. Personally, I've always been a fan of monosyllabic words. They're the prime numbers of our language—indivisible except by itself and the number one—so these nuggets toughen up the structure. Makes it a rock. Makes it immutable. Second, I believe the *right word* should also be reflective of one's outlook and personality. We bond with words that tie to the persona we want our letters, and art, to reflect.

Here goes nothing—grist is my right word. Grist sounds like what is heard and felt when you bite down on a nut that's more shell than meat. Grist is the sound my knees make going up stairs, my heart feels when thinking about the future, and like a fowl's gullet and gizzard, grist aids in processing what gathers inside.

We all think of the phrase grist for the mill, which is something useful for a particular purpose: the struggle between change vs. the desire to stay the same. The metaphor of the grist mill is one of the breaking down the self in order to change the world for the better.

Grief, gruff, grit, grift, guilt—granted, these phonetic second cousins aren't flattering. That's ok, the writing life is not a beauty contest. Guttural resonance sometimes feels so satisfying, and they are good words to pull out when necessary.

Grist is the grain separated from chaff in preparation for grinding. Metaphorically, our hours are all grist. Grist for me is indeed a hard nut to crack, just like writing. Vamos, amigos, let us all find our individual *right word* and sew it into the lining of our Monday night neckties.

Finally, there is a right word for right now: finito. Bonne nuit, Madam Calabash.

Gratefully oblivious that a lifetime of keeping one's nose buried in a book might lead to a career, **RICHARD HUNT** works as president of AdventureKEEN, a book publisher specializing in nature, regional, outdoor recreation, and children's titles. Retribution to that charmed beginning is a life sentence/side hustle as stevedore/owner of Roebling Books & Coffee in Covington and Newport. Way back when, after graduating from the University of Dayton, he was recipient of the first Oscar Dystel Fellowship in Book Publishing at NYU. Thereafter, he worked at Bantam Doubleday Dell in NYC, Houghton Mifflin in Boston, and F&W Publications in Cincinnati.

Chicago Literary Club's Sesquicentennial Chairman Jim Thompson and CLC President Robert Jordan welcome Richard Hunt and Mark Motley from the Cincinnati Literary Club,

Tentative Histories

Near the beginning were the handicrafts
of pot and bowl, hallowed
apportioners, sacred containers,
stone chalices more ancient than pyramids.

And then the blessing of rings and
bracelets, and the grand queenly
pectorals of lapis lazuli or jade,
fit to be buried with.
And thus, inevitably,
since so much else to see,
the varied epiphanies of scopes—
teles, micros, laporos —
Galileo, Van Leeuwenhoek, the surgeon of my kidney.
We know what we are doing
when we follow our hands and eyes
into craft,

when we genuflect among the shards
to sharpen the obsidian point
with one keen haptic move,

when we kneel beside the garden
confident, firming soil over seed,

when, blessing ourselves for luck,
we plunge toward the end of the poem
in hopes of the perfect genius of a word.

– RICHARD HAGUE

8

My Uncle's Legacy

RICK KESTERMAN

Arriving at my late uncle's house, I pulled my car over to the curb, put it into park, and stared out the window. Even though I had been here dozens of times before, this visit was filling me with a certain misgiving about what was now expected of me. I had decided to park on the street rather than the driveway so that I might not draw as much attention to my being there. I didn't relish the sympathy of neighbors I had rarely met, or frankly care for what I considered to be just too many nosey questions.

Feeling the need to procrastinate, I took my supplies and coffee out of the car, walked around to the back of the house, and sat down on a patio chair. Looking out at the garden, I thought about how I played in the yard years ago when my parents would come for a visit. The sounds of birds and insects were prominent, with only the faintest sound of traffic and lawn mowers in the distance. The warmth of the sun and coffee soon calmed me down, making my task for the day seem a little less formidable. After all, I didn't need to complete anything today, I just needed to make a reconnaissance, so to speak, of where my uncle's financial affairs stood.

Becoming more stoic about the day, I walked around to the front of the house and let myself in. It's strange just how different an empty house with the curtains closed is from the same structure when it is occupied. I usually don't mind being alone, but this time I would have loved to have heard my uncle tell me an amusing story or joke to break the tension I was feeling. Turning on some of the lights helped a little, and seeing the furnishings calmed me down as well. My aunt and uncle loved to travel, and as such had amassed a collection of postcards, brochures, and souvenirs that were lovingly stored in labeled boxes and binders throughout the house. In addition, photographs by my aunt and pen and ink illustrations by my uncle adorned most of the walls.

Settling down in my uncle's study, I searched his desk for the key to the small file cabinet that was next to the desk. Unlocking the cabinet, I opened the top drawer and began my search. With a precision that seemed alien to me with my own files, all of his financial records were organized in well marked folders, so that in only a couple of hours, I had most of the information that I had come to get. Since this task had been accomplished rather quickly, I decided to see what was in the other two desk drawers. The middle drawer contained packets of old invoices along with several folders of old catalogs. The bottom drawer was more interesting, as it contained items of a much more personal nature. Normally I would have just ignored them, but given my present circumstances, I decided I should take a few minutes to go through them.

Warming up to the task, I decided to liven up the room a little by opening the curtains to let in some natural light. I don't remember the last time I saw this room so bright, but it filled me with a renewed energy as I began looking at what had been saved through the years. Some of the folders related to trips, while others contained correspondence relating to illustrations he had been commissioned to produce; however, the folders that interested me the most were the ones that contained notes and papers concerning his college education.

One thing I hoped to find was some additional information concerning an incident that had taken place during his sophomore year when he was studying printmaking. According to family stories and a brief newspaper account that my parents had kept, one weekend, my uncle was busy etching a zinc plate when a fire broke out in the room near to him, possibly due to faulty wiring. Unable to locate a fire extinguisher, he attempted to smother the flames with his coat until he passed out from the smoke and fumes of the fire. An instructor who was in a room down the hall heard the commotion and raced to the scene, pulling my uncle to safety and then extinguishing the flames. Fortunately, the damage to the room was minimal, and no one was seriously hurt. My uncle fully recovered and received something of a hero status due to his prompt attention to the crisis at hand.

I don't know what I had hoped to discover, but I was disappointed to find that there was literally nothing I hadn't already seen concerning the events of that day. I guess that shouldn't have surprised me much since my uncle almost never spoke about the incident; in fact, he rarely spoke of anything serious, preferring to concentrate on more enjoyable or humorous aspects of his life.

Reading through these papers took a lot more time than I expected, and after looking at them for a few hours, I thought that I should take a break and get something to eat. Before leaving, I decided to straighten up some of the papers I had left on the desk. Having refiled the folders, I locked the file cabinet and opened the top desk drawer to return the key. Looking in the drawer, I saw a large envelope with my name on it that I had overlooked earlier.

It seemed strange that as methodical as he was in his record keeping, he would have simply left something lying in his desk drawer for me to find this way. I opened the envelope addressed to me and removed the contents, which consisted of a half dozen handwritten sheets of paper along with a small white envelope. The first page was to inform me of my being appointed as the executor of his estate, while the remaining pages contained a description of where he kept his records, along with other details I might need to know.

So far, it appeared that he had intended to mail this to me and never got around to doing so. All that remained was the small envelope, which was blank except for the word "personal." Opening the envelope up, I found several pages that seemed to have been written at different times, the first page being the most recent.

My dear nephew,

In the file cabinet by my desk, you will find a file marked donations. It contains, among other things, some receipts for contributions that I have made to my college for many years. These contributions were made both in appreciation for the education I received, as well as to make amends for something I had done. I know that you are aware of the story of the fire at my school, but here are some additional facts that I have kept hidden since that day.

At the time of the fire, most people came to the conclusion that it was started either from some older wiring or from a faulty extension cord. This was a natural assumption since most of the art rooms at that time were in some need of repair, but what actually happened was quite different.

I had an assignment in my printmaking class that was taking more time than I had anticipated, and so I decided to go to the classroom one Saturday to hopefully get caught up. I was making some real progress, and while I was etching my last plate, I decided to enjoy a cigarette, since I thought that I was alone in the building. I was almost finished with the cigarette when I heard someone in another room and realized that I would be in trouble if I didn't get rid of it right away. I quickly tossed it into what I thought was an empty can next to the etching cabinet, not thinking that it was for the rags that had been used to wipe up solvents.

As soon as the cigarette hit the rags, they were ignited, and flames shot up from the can. I grabbed my jacket and tried to smother the fire, but the smoke and fumes soon got the best of me and I passed out. The fire had destroyed what was left of the cigarette, and the smoke from the fire hid any trace of my own smoke.

No one ever thought I was responsible for the fire; in fact, I was even praised for my futile efforts in attempting to put out the blaze. At first, everything seemed to be fine; however, as time went on, it became progressively more difficult to reveal the truth, and I became more and more disgusted with the undeserved attention I received.

Although this isn't in my will, I would like one last donation to be made from my estate, and if the college would want them, you can donate any of my papers, including this letter, to their archives.

– Your uncle

For a few minutes I sat and processed what I had just read. I could kind of understand his not having said anything to his father or mother—after all, my grandparents could be rather stern at times—but certainly he could have told my father, and did he actually keep this secret from his wife all those years? As I thought about it, I realized that even though his confession might have altered my feelings about him a little, the change was, for the most part, a positive one. His actions in fighting the fire that day were still heroic, even if the fire had been simply caused by his own negligence.

Getting up from the desk, I went into the living room and idly began looking at some of the souvenirs and boxes on one of the bookcases. After rummaging through a box for a while, I made up my mind as to what I needed to do. My uncle's art and travels were his legacy, not some incident that happened over sixty years ago. I would see that his papers were offered to his college, and after the estate was settled, some monetary donation would be made to his memory.

Returning to the study, I picked up my papers and the small envelope and headed for the front door. As I grasped the door knob, I realized I had one last task to do that day. Picking up my uncle's lighter by the side of his ashtray, I went outside to the fire pit, lit a corner of the confession, and dropped it in the ashes as it met the same fate as the cigarette had so many years before.

RICK KESTERMAN is a lifelong resident of the west side of Cincinnati, and has been a member of the Literary Club since 2006. His experiences have spanned a variety of fields since he received a Bachelor of Fine Arts from the Art Academy of Cincinnati in 1983, including time teaching elementary school art and working with libraries and archives. His interests include travel, nature, and history.

9

Hope in Hell

MICHAEL H. KREMZAR

This paper is a tribute to a man whose memory continues fresh in my daily thoughts even though he died in 2002 at age 85. Ernest Gordon was Dean of Chapel at Princeton University for 17 years starting my freshman year. His unique background gave him the perspective and grace to sustain and strengthen an entire university. An unusual claim but a most unusual man.

Born and raised in Scotland, Ernest Gordon joined the Argyll and Sutherland Highlanders infantry regiment as an officer at age 22 in 1938. The Argylls maintained a strong Scots sense of the glory of battle and prided themselves as being the first to a fight and the last to leave. By 1941, Ernest was a Captain based in Singapore but stationed up-country in Malaya.

On December 8, 1941, the British Commonwealth forces in Malaya were surprised and quickly driven back by landings of 125,000 Japanese troops in Malaya and Burma (now Malaysia and Myranmar). The timing was simultaneous with the Japanese air attack on United States naval facilities and ships of war at Pearl Harbor—December 7 on the other side of the International Date Line. Many Americans, then and now, focused on the tragedy of Pearl Harbor and did not appreciate the much larger attack on the other side of the world. Although these two battles prompted declaration of war by both the United States and Britain, the start of WW2 really began earlier with the Japanese invasion of China in 1937. This Malayan invasion was a continuation of the Japanese plan to completely isolate and control China as well as protect sources of raw materials. As an aside, the current government of China is building a world class military capable of preventing any other nation from ever controlling this part of their world again.

The Argylls had been well trained in jungle warfare and inflicted heavy casualties on the invading Japanese. However, the British had based their defense on Singapore as the "Gibraltar of the East" along with their forces in India. But they had not recognized the impact of air power supporting a well-planned invasion on many locations. By December 10 off the coast of Malaya, the modern battleship, HMS Prince of Wales, and the cruiser, HMS Repulse, had become the first warships to be sunk at sea entirely by air attack. Commonwealth and Malayan forces totaling 120,000 were driven down the Malay peninsula to Singapore island. A large earthen causeway supporting a two-lane road and a rail line connected Singapore to the peninsula. Captain Gordon was one of the three Argyll officers to be the last to cross the causeway as it was blown up behind them—upholding the Argyll image of "last to leave."

Singapore was doomed without any possibility of re-supply or even fresh water and the Gibraltar of the East was forced to surrender on February 15, 1942. British officers trapped in Singapore, including Captain Gordon, were encouraged to try to escape in any way possible before the surrender. In the confusion before surrender, Gordon met up with a British Colonel who was planning an escape by boat. With extraordinary inventiveness, a 50ft long coastal sailboat was acquired and provisioned with as much food and water as the boat could handle. A group of 10 including Captain Gordon made their desperate try for freedom by setting sail in the direction of Sumatra. After weeks at sea, they barely managed to reach a small island off the coast of Sumatra and were able to replenish supplies and patch their battered sail. The Japanese were in the process of occupying Sumatra, so the intrepid sailors, valuing freedom over safety, set sail for Ceylon (now Sri Lanka) over hundreds of miles of open ocean. Their little boat was spotted by Japanese ships and their arduous three-month journey for freedom ended. The return to Singapore was an inglorious trip on the deck of a Japanese supply ship.

Once a thriving city that they last saw in flames, the Singapore in May 1942 was a dead city with few signs of life. The battle for Singapore had been ugly by any standard. The Japanese were carrying out a policy of systematic killing of ethnic Chinese and anyone who was suspected of resisting the invasion. This included the massacre of doctors, nurses, and patients at Alexandra Hospital on February 15, 1942. The atrocities inflicted by the Japanese during their occupation of Singapore are remembered there today.

Gordon and the rest of the sailboat crew were placed in a POW camp with 60,000 other Commonwealth military. The Japanese provided about 12 oz of polished rice per day and nothing else. The men in the camp had to survive on their own. Oil drums were made into cooking pots, tin cans fashioned as drinking cups, and medical supplies scrounged from unknown sources. Any prisoner who did not sign a "no escape" document was isolated and starved into either signing or death. A small, short-wave radio had been smuggled into the camp, but the news continued to be bad. Punishment for listening to the radio was severe. Five soldiers caught listening were stomped to death under the direction of a young Japanese officer—a recent graduate of Columbia University.

A high fever struck Gordon and was diagnosed as a form of malaria. With no medicines, he sweated out this attack without the aid of atropine or anything else. After he recovered from that bout of malaria, he developed stomach and intestinal problems which were diagnosed by a doctor among the POWs as a combination of intestinal worms and inflamed appendix. The appendix was removed while he lay on a kitchen table with a few drops of ether dropped onto a pad over his face.

While recovering, Ernest Gordon was among the POWs moved to camps in Thailand and Burma as slave labor along with conscripted Asians. The Japanese used them to build a 250-mile railroad from Bangkok to connect into India. The route was impossible to comprehend - passing through massive bamboo jungles, mountains, rivers, and huge gorges. Approximately 60,000 Commonwealth POWs and well over 150,000 locals were moved to work camps along the route. To prepare you for the description of Ernest Gordon's life in those camps, compare the less than 4% (1-2% US and 3-4% British) mortality of US and British prisoners held by the Germans during WW2, often in harsh conditions, with the 30-40% death rate in Japanese control. Here is a quote from Ernest Gordon: "During the years that they were in control, the Japanese military violated every civilized code. They murdered prisoners overtly by bayoneting, shooting, drowning, or decapitation; they murdered them covertly by working them beyond human endurance, starving them, torturing them, and denying medical care."

The prisoners heading to work on the railroad were transferred though various camps either by being packed standing up in railcars and barges, or walking carrying construction tools. The destination of a large group including Captain Gordon was a camp called Changkai located where the Kwai River passes through a steep gorge. The POWs built their own huts to Japanese specifications using bamboo and grasses. The immediate destination of this part of the railroad was to build a bridge over the river—well known now as the 'bridge over the River Kwai.' Their work started at dawn every day of every week and every month cutting the jungle and preparing the foundation for the railroad—hauling dirt and rocks using baskets and bare hands. Then carrying timbers from the river to build this bridge only with their hands and backs. The guards were increasingly belligerent to meet an impossible schedule of completion. Their main English word was "speedo" shouted or screamed along with beatings with bamboo rods or rifle buts. Rations were about 12 oz of rice per day and all drinking water had to be boiled by the prisoners. There was no medical care except for the few POW doctors who could tend to patients with whatever tools or treatments they could invent. This heavy workload in the tropic heat went on for months with no hope for relief. Men became walking skeletons sweating under the sun clad only in loin cloths and besieged constantly by bugs of many varieties. Tropical diseases were rampant in these malnourished, exhausted men. Malaria, beriberi, dysentery, diphtheria, and cholera all swept through the camp. A separate hut was designated as "Hospital" for those who could not work but had some chance of recovery. Another hut became the "Death House" for those who likely would not be able to survive. The dead were usually buried in mass graves dug by the POWs. The cholera victims' bodies were stacked next to the river and burned in a macabre pyre.

With no obvious future besides endless torture and constant back breaking work, men lost hope. Thievery became common and suspicion about equal distribution of rations caused paranoia. The Japanese cooks would place the garbage cans from the guards' meals outside their mess tent, and POWs fought over the scraps like a pack of wild dogs. Prisoners became more like animals than men. The Japanese paid little attention to the life inside the camp and continued to hound the prisoners beyond human capacity. Their brutality increased, including an officer who was instructing POWs how to attach wires to explosive charges. As the POWs worked to finish the task, the officer calmly walked over to the detonator and pushed the plunger. The sight of men being blown up was a great amusement for the officer and the guards. Hope is a rare commodity in any prison, it became even more rare in a work camp controlled by cruelty in the middle of the jungle.

Without rank designations in the camp, Captain Gordon, became simply Ernie. His malaria returned and he became infected with amoebic dysentery. He started to have trouble controlling his legs and a large white mass blocked his throat indicating diphtheria. Ernie was moved to the Hospital with his mates trying to bring food to him. Although he had dug the white infected mass out of his throat himself, Ernie had trouble eating and his legs became completely paralyzed. It wasn't long until Ernie was moved to the Death House.

The living dead are not great companions. Ernie was on a bamboo mat with his feet nearly touching the head of someone who seemed to breath only occasionally. Other POWs acting as orderlies tried to keep the patients comfortable, but the hut was stacked with dying men receiving no medical care. Ernie could barely talk but convinced an orderly to carry him into the back room that served as the morgue. It was less crowded, and air could circulate a bit from the river. The orderly advised him to move some part of his body whenever someone entered lest he find himself in a slightly pre-mature grave.

Out of the darkness, a friendly face appeared. Although Ernie was not recognizable in his current emaciated state, Tom Rigdon was able to find him. Tom was a civilian businessman swept up by the Japanese and treated like a POW. He was bunked with the Argylls and came to get Ernie out of the Death House. The Argylls built a lean-to on the side of their hut so that Ernie could remain isolated but with friends close by. He was relieved to be in a cleaner shelter although he saw no hope of his own survival. Without any ceremony, one of the Argylls, Dusty Miller, came into his shelter ducking his head and squatted on the dirt floor. After some brief chatter, Dusty took inventory of Ernie's situation—particularly the open, infected sores on his paralyzed legs. Dusty became not only visitor, but also a nurse and spiritual advisor. Soft spoken but always an encouraging word for his adopted patient. His background was the equivalent of high school education, and his plan was to return to Newcastle to help his father in his small landscape business. Dusty had been assigned as a night worker in the Japanese kitchen and was able to slip added food to Ernie. Had he been caught taking anything out of the kitchen, he would have been killed. However, he concealed a bit of vegetable, an egg, and even a little more rice hidden under his loin cloth. Equally important was the small amount of salt that he boiled in water to clean the open sores on Ernie's legs. Dusty worked without complaint cleaning puss from Ernie's wounds every day. Another Argyll, Dennis Moore, called Dinty, became a regular visitor. Dusty could treat Ernie during the day and Dinty would arrive at night. Where Dusty was quiet and thoughtful, Dinty was an ebullient spirit who always seemed to have a joke, story, or just a smile ignoring the horror around him,

These two men not only gave Ernie some hope of recovery, but also provided unguarded conversation. The most important discussions were about the meaning of life in a situation where human life was degraded. The two key questions from Erne were: why are you helping me and why do you have such hope for my recovery? Ernie heard the heartfelt descriptions of Christian faith by his two caregivers. Dusty was a Methodist and Dinty a Roman Catholic, but neither had any deep knowledge or concern about theological ideology. Both were acting out what they understood to be basic to the teachings of Jesus—love your neighbor. Their hope was not in their existence at the hands of the Japanese, but the promise of love from Jesus now and life after death. They did not waste time or energy hating the Japanese who, to them, were simply a very unpleasant environment. Ernie was moved by this personal image of living faith through action and the comfort of realizing that there was nothing the Japanese could do to him that affected his soul.

Dusty massaged Ernie's legs daily for weeks and his wound cleaning facilitated healing, so he fashioned a bamboo crutch and virtually forced Ernie to his feet to start walking. Few painful steps at a time over weeks, Ernie became a human again walking on his own. His main remaining physical problem was the amoebic dysentery that forced him to the slop bucket every hour and a half—day and night, Unknown to Ernie until years after the war, his friend Tom Rigdon had managed to keep his gold Rolex watch through almost two years of captivity. There was a secret "black market" with the local villagers where the prisoners could trade items like pens, combs, and other trinkets for an egg, a piece of fruit, or even some medications. Tom traded his gold Rolex for 11 doses of the medicine, Emetine—the minimum dosage for treating dysentery. The Emetine did its job, and Ernie was at last free of the debilitating effects of dysentery although still recovering from his appendectomy, intestinal worms, malaria, and diphtheria.

A heavily used Bible fell into Ernie's hands, and he started regular reading. Based on a discouraging experience in college where he attended a seminar on Christianity that started with the Book of Leviticus, Ernie decided to focus just on the New Testament. To his surprise and consternation, an Australian POW came to him and asked if he would lead a Bible discussion with his mates. Ernie's protestations about lack of knowledge or credibility were calmly ignored by the Aussie. Ernie found himself on the edge of camp one evening with this small gathering. The group grew to the point that other small groups started. Also, a worship service began on a regular basis on a corner of the camp that became known as "The Church." The POWs were not "typical" church people. Many of them including Ernie had killed men in battle and thought that they were being punished by God in this jungle hell. Christians to them were a closed-minded group that looked down on others, had rules and regulations, and saw the enjoyments of life as sinful. In Ernie's words, they saw Christians as people who extracted the bubbles from the champagne,

Ernie became one of the worship leaders and focused on the key themes he found in the New Testament. The apostles were men like them. They had nothing, were persecuted, tortured, and killed by the Romans, but continued to have hope and faith in a life everlasting. Any sins felt by the POWs were forgotten, and the current agony could be endured. The key message of "love your neighbor as yourself" resonated as something they could do—even in their suffering. About this time in the second year of captivity, men in the camp were starting to be aware of some examples of buddy helping buddy. In one well discussed example, an Argyll voluntarily took the blame for an alleged missing shovel to save the lives of the rest of his work group. His murder by the guard was made more dramatic when it was discovered that the guard had simply miscounted. Another POW had starved himself to provide food to a sick buddy. The patient survived but the friend died of starvation. Gradually, a spirit of hope and fellowship developed from the rock bottom of despair. Small classes in subjects remembered by an individual became active studies for men with no previous desire for learning. Subjects like philosophy, mathematics, golf, and various languages became important mental diversions. Ernie taught Greek with vocabulary on scraps of paper scrounged from old magazines or leaflets. An orchestra was organized with bamboo woodwinds, tea boxes and dried animal guts for string instruments that produced passable classical music. These and other stories marked a real turn of attitude and morale during this second year of brutal labor that coincided with the renewed interest in faith and hope. Although Dusty and Dinty were only two among many whose actions illuminated the message, their tireless ministrations to a near-dead Ernie were his return from darkness to light.

The Railroad of Death was finished in late 1943. An astonishing feat made tragic by the deaths of 16,000 POWs and 80,000 conscripted Asians. This represents a toll of 64 POWs per mile and 320 conscripted Asians for every bloody mile. With the completion of the bridge and railroad, the workload at Changkai changed to a more orderly ordeal. The work of maintaining the bridge and roadway was still physical and difficult but without the need for sunup to sundown work teams. The Japanese converted Changkai into a transit camp for prisoners being moved from work camps up-river. Any POWs that appeared to be able to perform hard work were transferred by ship to Japan. The Japanese refused to mark these ships with a Red Cross to indicate POW's. Some were sunk by Allied submarines since they appeared to be regular Japanese troop ships. Those POWs including Ernie who had illnesses or physical problems were sent to a camp, called Nakawm Paton, further down river.

Nakawm was a camp of sadness and despair. There were separate huts for different illnesses—although there was no medicine provided. One hut was designated for cases of amoebic dysentery, another for beriberi, one for tropical ulcers, and two behind separate barbed wire enclosures—one for leprosy and another for those who had gone insane. With the burden of illness and death, the ordeal of the past two years had worn down the camp into isolated, discouraged men with little physical or emotional energy remaining. Many had lost the ability to walk and had no hope of living long enough to care. Many of those arriving from Changkai, including Ernie, started massage teams that would go from man to man and massage their legs and talk with them. Ernie spent extra time with a farmer from Norfolk who continually rejected any help and was waiting to die. However, he was in no shape to stop Ernie from massaging his legs and talking to him. Over weeks of massage and leading the ex-farmer to talk about his wife and son, Ernie coaxed a glimmer of hope from the moribund figure. Following Dusty and Dinty's example, Ernie helped the farmer walk on his own—at least short distances. To many of the sick, the recovery of this one hopeless man was the strongest message of hope possible. The impact of the Changkai POWs on this woebegone camp was noticeable in cleanliness and hope during 1944.

Early in 1945 the POWs were aware that the Allies had bombed the bridge over the Kwai twice. Each time, the bridge was repaired with a combination of Asian laborers and POWs. Ernie and a group from Nakawm were sent back to Changkai to help repair the bridge. In June 1945, they were able to witness the successful destruction of the bridge by the RAF. During this air raid, the guards all scrambled to their designated bunkers, but the POWs climbed to a hill and cheered wildly as they saw the complete demolition of the hated bridge.

With the war turning against them, the Japanese began gathering the POWs into more central locations. Ernie was at a POW camp near Bangkok that was in the middle of Japanese army headquarters. One day, while hauling rock to reinforce a road, Ernie and his fellow POWs noticed that their guards had disappeared. After a short break in the shade, the POWs wandered back to the camp to find that there were no Japanese in sight. This was August 16, 1945, and the direct word of surrender from the Emperor of Japan via the Military High Command had reached this area quickly. The guards were afraid of the prisoners since they expected retaliation for the past three and half years of brutality. However, most POWs, including those with Ernie, felt strongly that they would not return evil with evil. They certainly did not greet the guards sneaking back with hugs and kisses, but they did not retaliate in any way. The timing of the sudden Japanese surrender on August 16 was unusually important. It was later learned that there was a general order to kill all POW officers the moment the Allies landed a force in Thailand. Since there was a scheduled RAF bomb run against the Japanese camp on August 17 and plans to land an Allied invasion force on August 28, the life and death balance for the POWs was precarious right to the end.

The now former POWs from around Burma and Thailand were transported in any way possible to Bangkok for medical aid and transport back home. Ernie searched every newcomer for any information about the two men who had labored so long and lovingly to bring him back to life—Dinty Moore and Dusty Miller. The news came in bits and pieces from men searching their memories for faces and names. Ernie's eager questions were finally answered by reluctant fellow ex-POWs. Dinty Moore was on one of those ships torpedoed on the way to Japan and there were no survivors. Dinty, that effervescent spark of life, died trapped in the hold of a sinking ship. Dusty was one of the POWs assigned to maintain part of the railroad. He was remembered warmly from a particularly dire camp. His calm demeanor in the face of insults and beatings so infuriated his guard that he crucified Dusty on a tree. This loving, giving spirit died like his Savior—a week before the surrender. Ernie never forgot these two men and the gift of life they gave to so many others.

The returning ex-POWs had similar difficulties as any returning combat soldier. They felt the shock of returning to a culture mostly concerned with possessions, status, and power. All missed the sharing, support, and a touch of the Eternal Truth that had developed with each other during the three and a half years of captivity. Many of those ex-POWs chose a future of service—teachers, ministers, medical aides, social workers. Ernie again became Ernest and chose ministry. He married his childhood girlfriend within three weeks of returning to Scotland and promptly was admitted to a hospital for 8 weeks of treatments for recurring malaria and a litany of other insults from his imprisonment. His diet was restricted for another two years and included a dose of hydrochloric acid with every meal since his stomach had lost the ability to generate digestive acid. Ernest followed through on his desire to build on his new faith and studied theology in Scotland and in the United States at Hartford Theologic Seminary. After returning to Scotland in a variety of roles, Rev. Gordon was invited back to the U.S. to fill an empty Presbyterian pulpit at small churches on Long Island—now with two children and his dedicated wife, Helen. His wartime experiences shaped his interests toward working with students, and that led to Rev. Gordon becoming Dean Gordon, the Dean of the Princeton Chapel.

As many of you know, the Princeton Chapel is a chapel in name only. The structure is a magnificent Gothic stone building that can seat 2,000 people with an organ that can shake the stones. As a religious symbol, it is non-denominational but, when Dean Gordon arrived, the

Sunday services were basic U.S. Protestant theology—now colored by Dean Gordon's Scots accent. The role of Dean of the Chapel is always ill-defined, but the Dean is tasked to coordinate the denominations on campus, preach most every Sunday in the Chapel, and represent the University in religious or morality questions not otherwise covered by the Religion Department. When he arrived in 1955, I was finishing my freshman year at Princeton. It wasn't until my senior year that I had the privilege of regular contact with him. A friend and I had scored that best job a scholarship student could find. We were caretakers of Murray Dodge Hall, the center for religious organizations on campus. Our duties were fairly simple, and we had a decent enough room on the top floor—with no room cost and a small stipend. Directly below our room was the Dean of Chapel's formal office with administrative staff. The Dean also had a small study nestled behind panels in the Chapel itself where he could go for quiet study and often meet with individual students who needed help with personal issues.

Dean Gordon's 17-year term as Dean of Chapel started with the "silent generation" of the 1950s and extended through the civil rights and Viet Nam war turmoil of the late 1960s and early 1970s. When he first arrived, his view of the student ethos was not particularly flattering. He saw the students of the late 1950's and early 1960's as entirely focused on Princeton as a gateway to a financially successful career. Many were following the direction set by their parents with expectation of degree and career choice pre-determined. From a faith standpoint, he observed a "dogmatic agnosticism" among students who were losing faith in the worship message of their younger years. The late 1960's and early 1970's hit the Princeton campus and many others with unrest including building takeovers. The students exploded with a new sense of freedom from old norms and rules of any type. Of all people, Dean Gordon understood what freedom meant and reached out to the students and to the university administration with a message that "freedom must be learned ...and earned." The long hair and shabby clothing of many students demanding change, were in form, no different than the Jesus he was preaching. That did not prevent a group of creative students from breaking into the upper vaults of the Chapel on a Saturday night so they could hang a commode over the pulpit. Dean Gordon was not particularly concerned about the commode except that it might drop at any moment while he was preaching. His understanding of the need for students to try to find out what freedom meant led him to remind the administration that "absurdity is one of the qualities of freedom."

During my early years a Princeton, I was a little scared of him. Any problems I had with short sleep, hard work, and tough competition for grades seemed too puny to bring to a man who had been tortured to near death for 3 ½ years! Even I could recognize myself as a whiny undergrad. However, his sermons were delivered in his crisp accent with a confidence that fostered attention. He would occasionally mention his time as a POW, but did not belabor it in his sermons. The message of "love your neighbor" and serve others came from his own life experience and not some fairy tale. During my senior year, I passed by his office area many times a day. He always greeted me warmly and we would talk about events on campus and life as I saw it. Of course, I discovered that he was a warm friendly guy who enjoyed chatting with undergrads—even a typical senior who knew the answer to everything

The students who came to him for personal counseling were similar over the years. Issues of being overwhelmed with the academic challenges, competition for grades, and anxiety about their future were common from the beginning. During the late 60s and early 70s, depression became more frequent among the students along with their desire for more freedom. The sense of freedom was great, but it weakened the moral compass that can support people in stress. Dean Gordon worked to help those who came to him to find that touchstone that was bigger than the events of this week or even this college career. He had seen men lose hope and die when others could survive with hope for their future and their faith in God. His style was not to say "now, now, it will all be all right in the end." Rather he would try to lead us to find what we really wanted with our life which may, this statement comes hard, just may be bigger than your four years at Princeton.

During my senior year, Dean Gordon took action that provoked some wide-spread attention—particularly from alumni. The nation was in the throes of civil rights turmoil with Black citizens, particularly in the South, demanding equal rights. The university was trying to balance the interests of alumni, faculty, and students with a careful posture. Dean Gordon stepped up and became a lightning rod by inviting the Reverend Doctor Martin Luther King, Jr, to preach in the Chapel on a Sunday morning in 1959. Many alumni and national newsmakers were not pleased and the letters to the alumni magazine and the administration were angry and, to many of us, embarrassingly racist. Unfortunately, Dr. King was injured in a personal attack and was not able to travel to Princeton at the arranged date. Alumni increased their ire when Dean Gordon announced that Dr. King's sermon would be rescheduled. Dr. King preached in the Chapel - June 1960. The letters and threats of cutting alumni donations continued for almost two years and beyond. Dean Gordon handled this brouhaha with calm confidence and reminded everyone of the University's motto: "Princeton In The Nation's Service." The President, Robert Goheen, was quick to defend and support the invitation. Dr. King delivered an eloquent message and was very well received by students and faculty. Later, he came to Princeton several times and made a major address in 1965. I was proud of the university and the administrations' strong support for Dean Gordon,

Dr. Martin Luther King Jr. and Dean of the Chapel Ernest Gordon, 1960. Princeton University Historical Photograph Collection

Dr. King, and the cause of freedom for all. As Dean of Chapel for almost two decades, Ernest Gordon helped lead and comfort the university and students with his unusual background and eagerness to serve others.

Searching my memory over these past six decades, it occurs to me that the one Princeton person I would like most to talk to again is Dean Ernest Gordon. He lived a life almost too full for any one person. I would like to know more about how he was able to forgive his captors in the jungles of Thailand and use that experience as stimulation to give hope to others. The message of concern for the students, citizens, and society he made into his life's work from the scars of captivity call out to me more now than ever. Words like hope and faith can be too familiar, but when combined with words like courage and conviction they became alive in Ernest Gordon.

Notes:

- *There are as many different names for locations as there are sources, e.g.: the bridge over the River Kwai was actually over the Mae Klong River. This paper stuck to the names used by Ernest Gordon. Also, the mortality figures vary by source but are all order of magnitude to the ones chosen in this paper.*

- *For your deeper understanding and reading, this paper was informed greatly by two books written by Ernest Gordon, "Through The Valley Of The Kwai" and "Meet Me At The Door," as well as "The Railway Man" by Eric Lomax.*

MIKE KREMZAR is an engineering graduate of Princeton University and saw Army duty before his career at Procter & Gamble, finishing as a Vice President—Global Product Supply. After his retirement, he co-authored a book titled "ERP: Making It Happen" (John Wiley & Sons). His recent focus has been serving on several boards of non-profit organizations that focus on helping people in need to build self-sufficiency, as well as writing fiction and non-fiction short stories.

Before the Founding Fathers, the Founding Families

ROBERT MULTHAUP

In 1683, the ideas that were to become the cornerstones of American values were neither conceived nor formulated. What became our founding ideals were forged from the thousand possible paths forward that emerged from the onslaught of peoples, cultures, religions, greed, and economic opportunities that blew in from a "bedeviled" Europe to the "pristine" shores of the American continent.

This paper is about the very early years of America, and the foundation of our ideals, when the destiny of one very small collection of souls first took a stand and conceived and communicated one of our most fundamental values: the abomination and the abolition of slavery.

We all have heard of the Mayflower that brought the first English-speaking Puritan peoples to the shores of Massachusetts. But very little has been publicized about the arrival of the Concord, which brought the first German-speaking colonists to Pennsylvania in 1683. Seeking religious freedom, these 13 families (33 persons in all) from Krefeld Germany, located near the Dutch border, were Mennonites turned Quakers, who had suffered severe religious persecution in their homeland. Ninety nine years before the founding fathers wrote the

Constitution and another 78 years before the 13th amendment finally abolished slavery, these families wrote the 1688 Germantown Petition Against Slavery which sparked a tiny flame which would eventually become a conflagration across the entire nation.

America is a place where the most extraordinary people have come from often modest beginnings, along with privileged elites who have forsaken their fortunes and found their voice to inspire change where they would have held their silence in the Old World. The story of how a small but extraordinary group of both wealthy and common settlers came to be the first evangelists of abolitionism is a complex tale of many influences: battling religions, the seemingly pre-destined crossing of paths of highly enlightened leaders, and the happenstance of the right people at the right time creating historic opportunity and circumstance. But, at the heart of the Petition Against Slavery, is the courage and bravery of the freedom-seeking families who left their homes and brought with them to America an entirely new set of values. The confluence of these social, religious, ethical, and human dynamics at a specific moment in time is the story of how a grandiose idea was born by the Krefeld families.

I discovered this relevant "outside the mainstream" history after I met my wife, Deborah Tyson. Her father had an interesting middle name, Reynier, which I hadn't heard before, and I asked its origins. It turns out Deb was a direct ancestor of Reinert Tisen (spelled many different ways), who was one of the original adventurers on the Concord that first settled in Germantown in 1683. He lived the events, experienced the trials and tribulations, and participated in the courageous moral stand that this small group of souls promulgated.

But beyond the lives of individuals like Reynier, there are four dimensions to this story that made possible the articulation of an idea that would become the first step in the American march toward freeing the slaves. These are:

• Deep character: religious persecution in Europe and America that drove humanistic beliefs—Mennonites, Quakers

- Leadership: the enlightened individuals who envisioned and forged a new path - Francis Daniel Pastorius and William Penn
- Freedom: the Germantown families who reclaimed their religious freedom there, and felt empowered to expand it to all
- Action: Pastorius and friends used this newfound freedom to speak their voice in the first anti-slavery petition

To better understand the anti-slavery petition of the Germantown settlers, it is necessary to position it within the social and religious context of the times they were living in. It can take a persecuted community, through the experiences of their own wounds, to build the personal integrity and moral courage that is required to stand up for one's true beliefs against a world that denigrates and even demonizes these beliefs. The Mennonites and Quakers, following the Thirty Years War, were constantly persecuted - always the target of both the mainstream Catholics and also Protestants who disparaged them for their deviant ideas and challenged their orthodoxy.

The historic crucible from where the beliefs and conscience of the Germantown settlers was forged begins in 1536 with a Catholic priest named Menno Simons. Simons left the Catholic church and became an Anabaptist because he believed in the doctrine of adult baptism. He experienced religious persecution culminating in the death of his brother and another man whose only "crime" was to be rebaptized. Once radicalized, his charismatic nature and religious conviction lifted him to become the leader of the Mennonites. He travelled throughout the Netherlands, Switzerland, and Germany as a hunted man, preaching nonviolence, adult baptism, and faithfulness to the Bible.

The Mennonites did not emerge unscathed from the Thirty Years War following the Peace of Westphalia (1648). Although religious equality was granted to major churches in Germany, it did not provide legal status or recognition to the Mennonites.

The Quakers suffered a similar fate as the Mennonites. Quakers were the followers of George Fox (1624–1691) who believed that true spirituality came from God speaking directly to the human soul through the "inner light" of the Holy Spirit. This belief sent Fox on a personal journey that led to the founding of a religious movement known as the Religious Society of Friends, or Quakers.

George Fox was imprisoned multiple times between the 1650s through the 1670s. His crimes were based upon: first, the Quaker Act 1662 which made it illegal to refuse to take the Oath of Allegiance to the Crown, and second, the Conventicle Act 1664 which reaffirmed that the holding of any secret meeting by those who did not pledge allegiance to the Crown was a crime. In the face of these threats, Friends continued to meet openly. These acts of defiance were testimony to the strength of their convictions and would imbue the future settlers of the new world with a strong will to seek religious freedom and freely express their beliefs. Mennonites and Quakers, to escape persecution, fled to America.

However, the lack of religious freedom in Europe was not ameliorated once in America. In 1657, while some Quakers were able to find refuge to practice in Providence Plantations established by Roger Williams, other Quakers faced persecution in Puritan Massachusetts. In 1656 Mary Fisher and Ann Austin were considered heretics because of their insistence on individual obedience to the Inner Light. They were imprisoned. They were banished. Their books were burned. Their property was confiscated. Finally, they were deported by the Massachusetts Bay Colony. Many other martyrs were severely punished. These events are described by Edward Burrough in "A Declaration of the Sad and Great Persecution and Martyrdom of the People of God, called Quakers, in New-England, for the Worshipping of God (1661)".

The end result of the persecutions of the Mennonites and Quakers in both Europe and America had the counter-effect of creating a very moral, strong-willed, and blatantly outspoken class of religious individuals who would not be silent in the face of injustice given their strong sense of righteousness.

These Quakers from Krefeld had difficulty reconciling the inhumane condition of the slaves in their new land. More than any other religious group at the time, they spoke up against the unequal treatment of any people based upon the color of their skin, because every person held the inner light. Their character, forged from their own persecution, could not remain silent in the face of slavery in their land.

Behind most transformational events are a few great leaders who combine their exceptional qualities into a mix of energy and purpose to elicit change. The two great forces that converged in the colony of Germantown were the freedom-loving vision of William Penn and the powerful personality and moral leadership of Francis Daniel Pastorius. William Penn's vision for the colony of Pennsylvania (founded in 1682) was a place where people from any country and faith could settle, free from religious persecution. Penn was a Quaker and a friend of George Fox. Because Penn's father was owed favors from King Charles II, Penn was granted the right to establish a proprietary colony with a democratic system of government with freedom of religion, fair trials, elected representatives, and separation of church and state. He needed people with like-mindedness to lead and fulfill his vision.

Francis Daniel Pastorius was born in Windsheim, Germany to a family of elite officeholders. He received an exceptional education: studied Latin, French, and Italian, attended universities in Strassburg, Basel, Jena, and Nürnberg, where he earned a doctorate in law in 1675. He was a man of great intellect and diverse interests who wrote many books on law, medicine, and general knowledge topics, and was considered one of the most important poets of colonial times.

From 1660 to 1680, William Penn visited the Rhine valley and organized gatherings where they preached the Quaker testimony. This is where the two leaders, Penn and Pastorius, first crossed paths. Pastorius was seeking spiritual release from his lucrative but uninspiring practice with the local gentry, and he turned inward looking for a philosophical purity in his life. He was attracted to Penn's vision of a colony as a place where religious freedom would allow him to start a fresh life free from "libertinism and the sins of the European world." Together, the two men planned for the Concord's passage in order to realize these dreams. In 1683, Pastorius was commissioned by the Frankfort Land Company and a group of merchants from Krefeld, Germany to form a settlement in America. They purchased 15,000 acres in Pennsylvania from Penn, which would become the community we know today as Germantown.

The ideas of Penn and Pastorius needed a place to find fertile ground where they could seed and grow into a wider and wider movement with a common set of beliefs and ideals. The 13 original Krefelder families (including Reinert Tisen plus four of his sisters and their husbands) proved to be the perfect catalysts to cultivate these new anti-slavery ideas. Their characters were strong: they were Mennonites who had become Quakers, and because they had been persecuted in their own land, they understood the value of a community founded on religious freedom. Unlike Pastorius, they were not wealthy, but were skilled craftsmen, carpenters, weavers, dyers, tailors, and shoemakers, who in the first few years suffered tremendous hardships as did nearly all the first colonists. But in a few years they built a self-supporting settlement where they set up looms and soon were producing linen cloth that sold widely throughout the colonies. More importantly, they created a spiritual village where they experienced, for the first time, true freedom of religion, where each person was free to express beliefs without fear.

Germantown was founded along a Lenni Lenape trail four miles north of Philadelphia, between the Wissahickon and Wingohocking creeks. In 1688, a mere five years from arrival in this wilderness, the families of Germantown felt compelled to express their repugnancy at what they witnessed in the institution of slavery. A cadre of three Quakers, along with Pastorius, came together to be the first to express their common abolitionist sentiments against slavery.

In addition to Pastorius, Garret Hendericks, Derick op den Graeff, and Abraham op den Graeff petitioned the Dublin Quaker Meeting to make their voices heard. The men gathered at Thones Kunders's house (Thones' wife was Elin Teissen Doors who was Reinert Tisen's sister). As a prolific writer in many languages, Pastorius was the primary author of the document, written nearly 100 years before our founding fathers penned their founding documents. The table it was written on is now housed at the Mennonite Museum in Germantown. The petition was presented to the Germantown Meeting of the Religious Society of Friends, and further up to the Quaker governing bodies. But the Petition was too early to be accepted, even by the Quaker leadership: slavery was too deeply entrenched.

Slavery had become a deeply rooted economic reality in the Americas in the late 17th century, and had expanded to all states, not just the South. William Penn himself owned slaves. Quaker businessmen owned ships that worked the British/West Indies/American triangle, and wealthy Pennsylvania landowners purchased African slaves to work on their farms. The general zeitgeist around the world regarded slavery as an endemic spoil of both conquest and trade: and most societies saw no contradiction in owning slaves as an economic necessity, especially in the New World which offered massive profits predicated on labor that could only be acquired based upon a lifetime of servitude.

The Africans were not exempt from complicity in their role in this slave trade. As Professor Robert Harms writes in *The Diligent*: "The slave trade could not have endured for four centuries and carried nearly 12 million people out of Africa without the cooperation of a huge network of African rulers and merchants."

In Europe, in the 17th century, servitude in the form of indentured servants was ubiquitous and harsh (although its duration was limited, typically 4-7 years). Around one half of immigrants to the new colonies were indentured servants (this practice was finally abolished in 1917).

Of great concern at the time, the Barbary pirates in the 17th century were allied with the Ottoman powers and captured Christian slaves to be brought back to North Africa or Turkey. In that period observers estimated that around 35,000 European slaves were held throughout the 17th century on the Barbary Coast, primarily in Algiers, Tripoli, and Tunis.

By contrast, the German Quaker settlers had never owned slaves. They could not in good conscience reconcile their belief that every individual human carried the inner light, indistinguishable by race, creed, or gender, and the atrocities perpetrated on slaves were perceived as an injustice to all men and women and children of equal worth and stature.

To urge the Dublin Quaker Meeting to abolish slavery, the three Quakers and Pastorius employed a somewhat unconventional approach: Instead of firing up the arguments on purely religious grounds or arguing on sanctimonious moral superiority, they based their objection to slavery on the very humanistic reasoning of the Bible's Golden Rule, "Do unto others as you would have them do unto you. "It does not contain references to Jesus or God, but rather hypothesizes that every human, regardless of belief, color, or ethnicity, has rights that should not be violated. This argument to abolish slavery, based upon the principle of equality of all mankind, can be viewed as an original formulation of fundamental American values. Following is the lead paragraph containing the chief arguments within the document:

"These are the reasons why we are against the traffic of men-body, as followeth. Is there any that would be done or handled at this manner? viz., to be sold or made a slave for all the time of his life? How fearful and faint-hearted are many on sea, when they see a strange vessel,—being afraid it should be a Turk, and they should be taken, and sold for slaves into Turkey. Now [in] what [way] is this better done, [than] as Turks do? Yea, rather it is worse for them, which say they are Christians; for we hear that ye most part of such negroes are brought hither against their will and consent, and that many of them are stolen. Now, tho' they are black, we can not conceive there is more liberty to have them slaves, as it is to have other white ones. There is a saying that we shall do to all men like as we will be done ourselves; making no difference of what generation, descent or color they are."

In spite of this proclamation, the general consensus for the abolition of slavery did not become universal, even among Quakers who only reached unity on the issue in 1754.

Over the years, the 1688 petition was forgotten until 1844, when it was re-discovered and became a focus of the burgeoning abolitionist movement in the United States. After a century of public exposure, the original petition was misplaced and once more re-discovered in March 2005 in the vault at the Arch Street Meetinghouse. It currently resides within the Haverford College Quaker and Special Collections, the joint repository (with Friends Historical Library of Swarthmore College) for the records of Philadelphia Yearly Meetings.

Looking back, through the confluence of a unique historic combination of character, leadership, freedom, and action, the settlers of Germantown Pennsylvania were the first community in America to voice objection to the horrors of slavery. Through the leadership of Pastorius, arguments to abolish slavery, based upon the simple golden rule, became the first step in expressing the founding ideals of the American experiment. Even though the Petition was not immediately accepted by the powers of the time, it was a catalyst of change that resurfaced throughout the long anti-slavery struggle, and was never fully forgotten.

The best tribute one can make to the Germantown settlers, who in 1688 wrote the first Anti-Slavery Petition, is to recognize that this spark of humanity and conscience that they started lit the entrance of a new path forward. This became a very hard-fought journey of events and laws that over time would ultimately eradicate the scourge of slavery with the passage of the 13th Amendment 177 years later. The fact that this first expression of abolitionism can be attributed to the conscience of a small group of immigrants is a testament to how American ideals were born: not from the greed of the rich and powerful, but from the souls of a few courageous and moral people. These values can then spread into a nation of believers and laws. How the values expressed in the Anti-Slavery Petition grew from the founding families to our founding fathers, and from ideas into laws, can be seen in the following path that the founding families lit:

- 1688: The Germantown Anti-Slavery Petition
- 1780: Pennsylvania passed the "Act for the Gradual Abolition of Slavery": the Importation Halt act stopped the importation of new slaves into the state. Children born to enslaved mothers after the specified date were automatically free, but they had to serve a lengthy period of indentured servitude until they reached the age of 28 before gaining full freedom.
- 1790: the Pennsylvania Society for the Abolition of Slavery—headed by Benjamin Franklin (a Quaker)—submitted an anti-slavery petition to the First Congress.
- 1794: French Colonies, the National Convention abolished slavery in all its colonies.

- 1799: New York passed a law for gradual abolition: children born after July 4, 1799, to enslaved mothers would be born free.
- 1817: New York legislature ends two centuries of slavery within its borders.
- 1833: British Colonies, the Slavery Abolition Act: freed more than 800,000 enslaved Africans in the Caribbean, South Africa, and Canada.
- 1844: the Germantown Petition was "rediscovered," it's importance as the first written protest against slavery in the United States was recognized and it became one of the most important documents in the
- 1865: Abolition movement. The 13th Amendment officially abolished slavery in the United States.

BOB MULTHAUP is a former CIO who worked for several years in Europe and now runs his own IT business where he developed management software. He has written many papers on the digital revolution. He is a graduate of the Choate school, Brown University, with an MBA in finance from Fairleigh Dickinson University. His writing interests focus on American historical stories (his ancestors were original Cincinnati pioneers).

Impertinent

The word itself
has a kind of sassy feel
to it: what brats do,
or teenagers wild on sugar
and sexting. That TV boy
in the MAGA hat last year.

What are the opposites of compliance?
Are good manners any good?
Can coal be lied into clean?

On the mountainside, a forest
inverts itself and shows
a harum-skarum of roots. Fish flop onto
broiling summer interstates; bees lose themselves
in huggermuggers of Congress.

Nonsense prevails. Prayers turn inside out,
become curses in the mouths
of girl scouts. Upending
the container does not always
empty it:

Alleghanies blown up and gone,
good fortune now is spills of Arctic oil.

– RICHARD HAGUE

11

THE DOPE BAG

T. STEPHEN PHILLIPS

On March 24, 1990, the largest crowd ever for a high school basketball game, 41,000, watched Damon Bailey and his Bedford North Lawrence team win the Indiana state tournament championship.

According to Wikipedia, the five largest high school basketball gyms in the country are located in Indiana as are 14 of the largest 16.

In 1925, James Naismith, the inventor of the game, attended the Indiana state finals along with 15,000 other fans. Thousands had been turned away at the door. Naismith was amazed, and he wrote: "The possibilities of basketball as seen [in Indiana] were a revelation to me. Basketball may have been invented in Massachusetts, but it was made for Indiana."

Naismith invented the game in 1891, while he was teaching at the International YMCA Training School in Springfield, Massachusetts. He had been tasked with coming up with an indoor activity to keep boys engaged between football and baseball seasons. For a game he had in mind, he asked the school janitor to find two square boxes which could be used as goals. The janitor came back with two peach baskets

which Naismith nailed to a balcony railing in a school hall. The distance from the floor to the peach baskets happened to be about ten feet.

Naismith called his game "Basket Ball," two words, and he devised a set of 13 rules for the game. The original of his two page rules manuscript sold at Sotheby's for $4.3 million in 2010.

Soon after he devised the rules for Basket Ball, Naismith published an article introducing the game in the YMCA national newsletter, and the YMCA advertised a "descriptive pamphlet" on the "new and popular game" which was available by mail for ten cents. Naismith's article and the YMCA pamphlet, and the correspondence which followed, are credited with spreading the game across the nation.

Crawfordsville lays claim to being the birthplace of Indiana basketball. The story is that Nicholas McCay, a student at Naismith's YMCA school, brought the game to Crawfordsville. But, in lieu of using peach baskets for goals, he had a blacksmith forge two metal hoops to which he sewed burlap coffee sacks.

Although the object of putting a ball in a basket and determining the winner by the number of baskets made hasn't changed, other aspects of Naismith's game have changed dramatically over the years.

Under Naismith's rules, a player with the ball couldn't bounce or run with the ball. He had to either shoot at the basket or throw the ball to another player. Later, a single bounce was allowed but only by the player first tossing the ball above his head. Continuous dribbling came later.

Originally, a center jump followed each made basket, giving great advantage to teams with a tall player or a good jumper.

There was no set number of players on a team. After experimenting with teams of greater numbers, early games were primarily played with nine players on a team; later, five players became the standard team.

In the beginning, boundaries of play weren't defined, which sometimes led to chaos. Goals were often affixed to the bottom of a balcony, and to recover possession of a ball landing in the balcony, players would dash up the stairs or be hoisted up. Court boundaries were added in 1913.

Initially, the games were played with soccer balls. The first basketballs were produced in 1894 by a bicycle manufacturer. The original balls were laced balls which lost their shape over time.

Using peach baskets or burlap coffee sacks made for a slow game since after each made shot the ball had to be removed from the basket or sack, often by someone on a ladder. In 1912, open ended nets were approved to replace the peach baskets and coffee sacks.

Indiana was ripe for a new amusement when basketball came to the state. At the turn of the century, Indiana was mostly a rural expanse scattered with hundreds of small towns with small schools. The school was the unifying force and a source of pride for the residents of a small community, and the reputation of a town was inextricably linked to that of its school. Schools were distinguished by the strength of their athletic programs, and competition between communities was most often seen on the high school basketball courts. For most of the small schools, fielding a football team was out of the question. Baseball was a summer activity. Basketball, on the other hand, was played competitively in the winter, and the sport didn't interfere with spring planting and fall harvest seasons. It was inexpensive. Even the smallest schools could scrape together five-man teams. As a result, the game blossomed, and basketball became an integral part of the state's culture and identity.

A large part of the popularity of the game in Indiana was because of the state high school tournament. Until 1997, the tournament was a single class tournament in which schools of all sizes competed. From the late 20's through the 50's, approximately 800 schools competed each year in the tournament. The starting point was the sectionals—64 across the state. Communities vied for being designated host of a sectional by building large gymnasiums, and it was not uncommon for a gym to have a capacity greater than the entire population of the town in which it was located. The 64 sectional winners met in sixteen regional tournaments, and the 16 regional winners met in four semi-final tournaments. The semi-final winners met in a finals weekend of games in Indianapolis. For 41 years, the finals were played at Butler Fieldhouse.

A charm of the single class tournament was that every small school had a chance of beating the bigger schools. And it was the chance to win which the small schools wanted. The most memorable of the underdog wins in a state final was in 1954 when Milan, a town of 1,150, and a high school enrollment of 161, beat perennial powerhouse Muncie Central, with an enrollment of 1,600, by a score of 32-30. In the fourth quarter of that game, with the score tied at 30, Bobby Plump froze the ball unchallenged for over four minutes before hitting a 14-foot jump shot as time expired. The Milan story was captured in the 1986 film Hoosiers. Bobby Plump went on to play outstanding college basketball at Butler University and for three years with the Phillips 66ers of the National Industrial Basketball League, but it was that last second shot in the high school state finals which defined him. Later in life, he could be found spinning tales about the glory of Indiana high school basketball at "Plump's Last Shot," a bar and restaurant he and his son operated in Indianapolis, which featured a pork tenderloin sandwich as big as a Frisbee.

Author Greg Guffey identifies the 1940's and 1950's as "The Golden Age of Indiana High School Basketball" in his book by that name. And, for me, the story of basketball in Indiana is in the 1950's, before school consolidations, when every small town in Indiana had a high school and a high school basketball team. I grew up in such a town, Tennyson, population 300, with a high school of about 100 students. The school had no gym until 1952, and players practiced outside on a clay court carefully maintained by students and teachers. Once a week, the team practiced indoors at a real gym located in a nearby town, Chrisney, and home games were played there. The coach, Woodrow ("Woody") Collins would cart his team back and forth to practices and games at Chrisney in the back of his pick-up truck, covered with a tarpaulin to protect the boys from rain and snow and bitter cold wind.

Then, the goal of every young boy was to make the basketball team, and the prized birthday or Christmas gift was a Spalding basketball or a pair of Converse basketball shoes.

Basketball goals were ubiquitous - hung on the sides of barns and houses or on poles planted to hold a goal. Sounds of a ball bouncing or hitting a basketball rim or backboard could be heard in every part of the community, sometimes a solitary player trying to perfect his shot, sometimes, a pick-up game of one on one or two on two, sometimes boys playing the game of horse, H O R S E, or competing to see who could hit the most consecutive free throws, with eyes closed. Father against son or fathers against sons, the sons shooting jump shots and the fathers shooting the shots of their era — two handed set shots, one handed push shots, running hook shots, underhand shots. I remember so well many years of one on one and other basketball games with my Father, marveling at the accuracy of his underhand and running hook shots.

The father of one boy was a tobacco farmer who installed a wood floor in his barn and put goals inside at each end. When tobacco wasn't hanging to cure, the basketball barn was open for boys to use—a real "indoor" court.

Talk of each year's high school team dominated conversation at school, over meals at home, and in local establishments - particularly at Chester Broshears' barber shop and the gas station.

The Warrick county weekly newspaper and the Evansville dailies had extensive coverage of high school basketball. A sports reporter had near celebrity status, and young reporters could earn their stripes on the sports beat. One such young reporter for the Scripps owned *Evansville Press* was William R. Burleigh, whose media career culminated in service as president and chief executive of E. W. Scripps Co. At age 15, Bill began his newspaper career as a part-time high school sports reporter while attending Memorial High School.

All of which leads to this story of the Dope Bag.

The Dope Bag originated in the Fall of 1929, the brainchild of Franklin A. Hunt, sports editor of the then *Evansville Journal*. Hunt wrote a basketball column titled "Splinters Off The Hardwood."

He conceived the idea of having a trophy which would move from winning team to winning team in eight counties located in southwestern Indiana. The purpose of the Dope Bag, Hunt said, was to foster competition and better sportsmanship among teams in that area.

The Bag was just that - a large black leather satchel with carrying handles such as a traveler might have or that I remember being carried by our town physician, Doc Bruce, to hold medicines and instruments while making house calls.

The term "Dope" had a meaning different than we'd associate with the term today. It meant "inside" or special information. (You know, what's the dope?) Inside the Bag was a metal box containing a log of the teams that had won the Bag and descriptions of games in which the Bag changed hands.

Under Hunt's Rules for the Bag, a full account of each game in which the Bag changed hands was to be recorded in the log, including names of the winning and losing team captains and coaches, estimated fan attendance, and a description of sportsmanship exhibited at the game. A ribbon with the school name and colors could be placed in the Bag or tied to the handle of the Bag, and over time the Bag was stuffed with ribbons. A ceremonious exchange of the Bag was to occur at center court between the captains of the losing and winning teams. And the Bag was to be placed in the trophy case of the winning school or in the show window of a town store whose proprietor was a strong supporter of basketball.

When the *Evansville Journal* suspended publication in 1936, sponsorship of the Bag was taken over by the *Evansville Courier* sports column "Dribbling Around." The *Courier* was a competitor paper of Bill's *Evansville Press.*

The Bag became treasured among schools in the area, and the archives of the *Courier* are replete with sports page stories about the travels of the Bag, often with pictures of the winning team coach and players.

In mid-January, 1958, Woody Collins was at his desk between classes at Tennyson High School when Agnes Gentry, secretary to the Principal, told Woody that the Principal wanted to see him.

Woody taught typing and bookkeeping, but his main responsibility was coaching the basketball team. He had come off two mediocre seasons, and he was aware of the growing sentiment in town that he should be replaced. When Agnes came into his classroom, Woody had been replaying in his mind the last game, at Birdseye, wondering whether his standing as coach had risen because of the game. Tennyson had won, but the game was marred by an altercation between ardent Birdseye and Tennyson fans. One referee had been clearly favoring Birdseye, and mid-way through the third quarter, one of the Smith brothers came out of the stands and slugged the ref as he ran down the Tennyson side of the floor. A Birdseye fan came across the floor to do battle, the two other Smith brothers joined the fray, and for a minute or so a half-dozen angry men exchanged blows on the floor. The teams were hurried to the dressing rooms as the town sheriff marched onto the floor brandishing his pistol. Order was restored, blood was wiped from the floor, and the teams eventually returned to complete the game. Reports were that the Smith brothers stayed away from home for several days for fear of being arrested for their part in the melee.

Woody had been a loyal and active member of the Republican party at a time when teaching and coaching jobs were dispensed by and held at the grace of the Township Trustee who was then a Republican, Nolan Scales. Woody would have some leeway because of his political affiliation, but both he and Scales knew that an election could be lost over such a matter as keeping on an underperforming coach. The current season had been some better, and the team was five and three at that point. Respectable, but perhaps not good enough for a demanding town.

The Principal, Roy Barchett, who was called Principal Roy by students, was grinning ear to ear as Woody entered the Principal's office. Principal Roy was a short, rotund, nearly bald man who had a habit of clapping his hands loudly when he was excited or wanted to drive home a point. He clapped his hands as he stood from his chair and said loudly "Woody, I just got a call from the principal at Wadesville. They're holding the Dope Bag, and we'll be playing for it."

Woody grinned and clapped his hands as well. He knew instantly that more would be at stake than winning the Dope Bag when his Tigers took on the Wadesville Red Devils in ten days.

"We'll be playing for the Dope Bag at Wadesville, boys," Woody told his team at practice that afternoon. Over the excited yells of his players, he went on to say, "Some of you boys know when Tennyson last held the Dope Bag. It was 1932, just three years after the Bag started. There's a picture of that team with the Bag," he said, pointing to a grainy photograph hanging at one end of the gym, "and another picture hangs down at Check's," referring to Chester Broshears' barber shop. "Your Dad played on that team," he said to Jack Harrison, whose father Johnny was owner of the tobacco barn basketball court. "Your uncle, Abner Haas, was coach of the team, and your uncle Jack played on the team" he said to another player who nodded knowingly, proud of the mention of this important piece of family lore. All the boys knew about the 1932 team, which had been dubbed the "gymless wonders." Without a gym, the team had been able to compile a record over two years of only one loss in regular season play and making the regional finals one year.

Woody later remarked that in all his years of coaching he had never seen boys so excited. Word soon circulated in the school and town that the Dope Bag was at stake at Wadesville. A plan was devised by Johnny Harrison and three other former players to drive to Wadesville, circulate, and spark conversation about the upcoming game, hoping to pick up useful information about the Wadesville players and the team's style of play—size of the players, good and poor shooters, whether zone or man-to-man defense was played. The collected information was distilled and reported to Woody. Wadesville played mostly man to man but would shift to a two-three zone if called for. Most scoring came from one of the guards and the center, who had three inches on George Barton, Tennyson's center. The team was slow to get back on defense after a missed shot. Practices during the week before the game were marked with boys running faster, jumping higher, and scrimmaging more fiercely than ever. An extra practice was held on Saturday. From the information garnered about the Red Devils, Woody devised a new fast break play to take advantage of the reported slow retreat to defense and a new play he called the double pick designed to result in an easy layup for one of the guards.

A caravan of cars followed the team bus on the hour-long drive to Wadesville which was located in Posey County, two counties away. Some cars sported banners with the team logo, and horns blared as the cars passed through small towns on the way.

Wadesville was a larger community than Tennyson, and the Wadesville gym was larger than Tennyson's, It was filled to the rafters for the game. Most of Tennyson had come, and the Tennyson fans occupying the visitor's side of the gym nearly equaled the Wadesville fans sitting across.

The Right Word

Cheerleaders from both teams led their fans in spirited cheers, each side trying to out-yell the other. The Tennyson cheerleaders had created new cheers for the game. Chants of "We want the Bag, we want the Bag" were answered by Wadesville's "We'll keep the Bag, we'll keep the Bag."

In the locker room before the game, Woody gave a fiery talk to his players. "Boys, you know what bringing the Bag back to Tennyson would mean to our school and to the town," he said, "Play hard and play smart. No turnovers. Good defense. Strong on the boards. They have two scorers, Merrill at guard and Edwards at center. Merrill's your man," he said pointing emphatically at Russell Roth, "stick with him like butter on bread," and "George, you've got Edwards," he said to Tennyson's lanky center, "he's taller than you, so use your butt to keep him away from the basket." He stood and exhorted his team, "Now, let's go get the Bag!"

The fired up boys burst through the locker room door and onto the floor before their screaming fans.

Wadesville was formidable, a well-coached team that had lost only one game of the seven played so far that year, and Tennyson fell behind by four at the end of the first quarter. Woody called for the double pick on the first offensive play in the second quarter, and it worked. And shortly thereafter, on a missed shot by Wadesville, the new fast break play worked as well. Tie game. And the game remained tied at halftime. Woody delivered another impassioned speech in the locker room, and the boys were made to believe that the future of the school and town depended on their performance in the next sixteen minutes of play.

It was back and forth through the third quarter, and Tennyson was down by two to start the last quarter. Jim Saltzman, the team's leading scorer, picked up his fourth foul on a questionable call, and the Tennyson fans collectively held their breath.

Midway through the fourth quarter Tennyson finally got the edge and thanks to accurate free throw shooting, a couple of long bombs from Saltzman, and another successful execution of the double pick, Tennyson won the game by a score of 70—64. The Bag changed hands at center court. January 21, 1958, the day that the Dope Bag returned to Tennyson. Woody had made only one substitution in the game, to give Barton a breather. Only five Tigers made the box score: Saltzman, 25 points; Phillips, 22; Barton, 11; Martin, 8; Roth, 4.

Such joy. Principal Roy declared one day to be Dope Bag day at school, and Woody and the team were honored in a program in the gym. The school band played, half the basketball players picking up instruments to regale themselves. Congratulatory signs were posted in store fronts. For a day, Check reduced the cost of haircuts from fifty cents to a quarter. The remnants of the 1932 team hosted a dinner for the players at Faye's diner.

The *Evansville Courier* carried a story of the victory, with a picture of Woody and the team alongside an archive picture of the 1932 team.

The first defense of the Bag was at Spurgeon, also away. Principal Roy called his counterpart there to inform him that the Bag would be at stake.

The 1932 team had held the Bag for several games, and Woody located and read to his players *Courier* accounts of some of those games played 26 years earlier. He later said that there had been good preparation for the game, but the intensity of practice in defense of the Bag was less than that in pursuit of the Bag.

There was another huge turn-out for the game. The Spurgeon gym was smaller than Wadesville's. Fans squeezed together, and dozens stood.

There was a different feel to the game. Spurgeon, now, was on its quest to gain possession of the Bag. The game was close throughout. Spurgeon played a tight man-to-man, and the player guarding Saltzman was effective in denying him shooting opportunities. Spurgeon led by a small margin throughout the game and was ahead by two at half time and at the end of the third quarter.

With just eight seconds remaining in the game, and Spurgeon up a point, 71-70, Saltzman was fouled attempting a jump shot, and he stepped to the line to shoot two, a chance to take the lead for the first time in the game. Spurgeon called time out to ice the shooter. In the huddle, Woody told his team, "we've got this one, boys. Jim, just two more shots like the thousands you've made. After Jim makes the shots, George, you guard the throw in, and Buddy and Russ, you contain the boy who takes the inbound pass. Keep the ball on Spurgeon's end. No fouls." Jim made the first shot. Spurgeon called another time out. Sweat dropping from his face, Woody repeated his advice to the team. Silence enveloped the building when Jim stepped to the line for the determining shot. Swish. 72-71. The Tennyson crowd went wild. Tennyson would keep the Bag. Just hold on for eight seconds. Woody admonished his players from the sideline, "Tight defense, pressure in the front court. No fouls." The ball was inbounded, and Roth and Martin immediately double-teamed the player with the ball, who gave up his dribble and looked for an open man. Seconds passed. Suddenly, there was heard loud shouting from the Tennyson scorekeeper, "Start the clock! Damn it, start the clock! He didn't start the clock!" The Spurgeon timekeeper had failed to start the clock on the inbound pass, a mistake which hadn't been noticed for a few seconds. As the clock started, the player with the ball found a teammate, also on Spurgeon's end of the floor and heavily defended, but who was able to make three dribbles toward half court before launching the ball toward the basket. The building fell silent and the buzzer sounded while the ball was in flight. Swish. The scoreboard read Spurgeon 73 - Tennyson 72.

Pandemonium ensued. Tennyson fans emptied onto the floor and charged the scorer's table. Threats were made and fists were shaken. Woody feared a repeat of the Birdseye game, and he rushed his team to the locker room as did the Spurgeon coach with his team.

The Tennyson boys were distraught, most crying. Their trophy, the trophy of the school and of the town, had been lost in their first defense of the Bag. Principal Roy and Nolan Scales came into the locker room to console the players. They huddled with Woody away from the players, who slowly began to change out of their uniforms.

And then Principal Roy addressed the team. "Boys," he said, "we were cheated. No two ways about it. You won that game, and we've decided that we're not giving up the Bag without a fight. They'll be after the Bag, but we're going to march out of here and back to Tennyson with it. Your parents are out there waiting for us. I'll talk to them. When you're dressed and ready to go, George will carry the bag. The rest of you huddle around him, and I'll tell your parents to huddle around all of you when you come out. They'll play hell breaking through to grab the Bag. I'll tell the Spurgeon principal and coach what we're going to do, and I'll take them on myself if it comes to that. We'll get the Bag back to Tennyson and decide what to do from there."

With nervous excitement, the boys emerged from the dressing room as they were told, some with clenched fists, George defiantly clutching the Bag tight to his body. Few had left the gym, the Wadesville fans anticipating an exchange of the Bag. The parents circled the boys as they were told, and the pack slowly moved through the crowd across the gym floor to the exit door and out to the team bus which had been moved to be near the exit. The plan worked. There were angry shouts from Wadesville but no violence.

On the bus ride back, emotions among the boys were varied—anger at the failure of the timekeeper to start the clock, pride that the team and town had stood up for what was right.

The following day, Principal Roy summoned to his office, at noon, Woody, Nolan Scales, Doc Bruce, and Lowell Phillips, who had been scorekeeper for Tennyson and had sounded the alarm about the clock not having started. Principal Roy reported to the group that he had already spoken to the *Courier* sports editor about the game, that the editor had called the Spurgeon principal to get Spurgeon's side of the story, and that the editor had reported back to Roy that the *Courier* would abide by a decision of the IHSAA, the governing body for Indiana High School sports. Tennyson would have to challenge the head referee's report of the outcome, which was Spurgeon winning 73-72, by filing a protest.

By end of the week, a formal protest had been prepared, supported by affidavits from Woody, Principal Roy, Nolan Scales, and Lowell Phillips. All attested that there was at least a four-second lapse before the clock started after the inbound pass and that the buzzer sounded an instant after the ball left the shooter's hands. Affidavits were also obtained from the timekeeper, who acknowledged that he had failed to start the clock, and from the referee, who affirmed the same, but neither of them would estimate the lapse of time between the inbound pass and start of the clock.

An opposing narrative was filed by Spurgeon.

The *Courier* reported on February 1, 1958: "The score of the Spurgeon-Tennyson game Tuesday night at Spurgeon may be changed. Coach Woodrow Collins of Tennyson protested the game to the Commissioner of the IHSAA, stating that time had expired when Spurgeon made the basket that put it ahead, 73-72. Coach Collins told the *Courier* that the officials and timer agreed with him. Until the Commissioner rules on the protest, The *Courier* Dope Bag will be held in abeyance at Tennyson."

Little else was discussed in Tennyson in the days before the IHSAA announced its decision, which was printed in its entirety by the *Courier*:

"Following a game of basketball between Tennyson and Spurgeon, January 28 1958, at Spurgeon, Principal Roy Barchett of Tennyson protested that the clock had been stopped for an attempted free throw with eight seconds remaining and that the timer had neglected to start the clock immediately.

This was admitted by the official timer. Some 20 pages of reports were filed by the principals, coaches, timers, and referees on the case. As is usually the case in situations of this kind, the statements were very much in conflict as to just what did occur with reference to the playing time.

Referee J.A. Yeager (Evansville) stated that he approved the final score as Spurgeon 73—Tennyson 72.

Decision: After careful consideration of all the evidence on file the Board of Control approves the final score as Spurgeon 73—Tennyson 72. The principal of Spurgeon High School is directed to have a competent timekeeper on all home basketball games."

Gloom descended in Tennyson.

While the protest was pending, games were played at which the Bag would have changed hands, and the *Courier* decreed that the Bag would be held temporarily by each of the teams that would have held the Bag, the *Courier* sports columnist writing: "The Dope Bag will make more whistle stops than the C&ET railroad this week on a belated excursion around Warrick and Pike counties . . . getting the Dope Bag to the rightful owner has become as complicated as a soap opera love scene."

Tennyson gave up the Bag, but not before including in the Log an account of the controversy and placing in the Bag a red and white Tennyson Tigers ribbon that dwarfed all the other ribbons.

And so ended that saga of the Dope Bag. For the Tennyson basketball team, school, and community, a time of great anticipation, great joy, and then great disappointment.

Although high school basketball remains very popular in the state, the glory years of Indiana high school basketball came to an end with the consolidation of public schools in the 1960's. Tennyson lost its high school as did hundreds of other small schools, and, later, the single class state tournament was divided into four classes. Another Milan story in Indiana became no longer possible, and the Dope Bag tradition ended as well. But, back at Check's, now called Tony's because Check's grandson is the barber, there hang photos of the 1932 gymless wonders and of the 1958 team, to remind those coming for a cut that Tennyson once had a high school and twice held the Dope Bag.

STEVE PHILLIPS grew up in small town Indiana, graduated from DePauw University and Duke Law School, and came to Cincinnati after graduation to join the Frost & Jacobs law firm. He currently practices with the Strauss Troy law firm.

12

Dinner at Irk's

G. JAMES SAMMARCO

City on a Bluff

Fort Lee, New Jersey, in 1975, a borough of thirty thousand people lay above the Hudson River opposite New York City, adjacent to the George Washington Bridge. It sits on a mass of igneous magma, hardened to a stony bluff 250 million years ago, 400 feet above the water, forming vertical cracks as it cooled, that looked like columns, from which it got its name, the Palisades. The riverbank was dotted with parks and marinas. Apartments and warehouses crowded in, with towns like Weehawken, Alexander Hamilton's fatal duel site, and Hoboken, Frank Sinatra's birthplace and his first arrest for soliciting a prostitute. Downstream the river broadened into Upper New York Bay.

Blue-collar workers, white-collar workers and executives, lived there commuting to New York City daily. The population was first and second-generation Italian, Irish and German, with others of varying ancestry. Pizzerias, trattorias and restauranti dotted the streets a few blocks from the GWB serving customers who lived near or drove in for dinner. Restaurants bore names, Trattoria Fratelli Baggi, Enzo's, Carmine's, Luka's, One trattoria "Uno-Otto-Nove" (No.18), another, "Pizza Always!"

and Baccigalupo's Italian Cucina, proudly displayed Italian fare, though few had ever been to Italy. Restaurante Lido Harlem, gave homage to Dutch settlers of New Amsterdam, serving Sicilian sausage and peppers, and Fume Harlem Trattoria next to a Dutch machine shop that belched smoke into the street. Smoking was permitted inside too.

One small restaurant, missed if not for its name, was "Irk's", emblazoned on the front window in six-inch gold letters. In smaller letters below, was Cucina del Sud Italia, (Southern Italian Cooking). New customers were confused. They wondered if "Irk's" referred to the quality of food. Originally a Hofbräuhaus, it closed in the Depression. An old German remembered the owners shortened their name from "Irkenbreckeren" when they landed in New York in 1923. He described them as "stuffy". They spoke Schwabisch dialect. The word "stickig", "wie das Englische Denken. Ist vas Ehr verkürzter Nachname", he said, "Ich erinnere mich." (like the English think, I was your shortened surname". I remember."

I grew up in Maywood, eight miles west. For fifteen years college, medical school, graduate training, fellowship and Uncle Sam occupied my time. I then joined an orthopaedic group in Cincinnati. I was at Columbia Presbyterian Hospital preparing for "examinations" to certify in orthopaedic surgery. I stayed with my parents in Maywood, a convenient commute to the hospital. On Wednesday my father phoned me, "How about dinner with Lou Zola and Bill Krause tonight? The restaurant is near your hospital, just across GWB."

Lou Zola was my father's mechanic and Bill, Chief of Police in Rutherford, longtime friends, with others, were having a "men's night out". I knew them and this was an invitation to a good Italian meal. Dad picked me up on the Jersey side of GWB at 7:00 PM.

"Uncle Jim is coming, pointing to him. He hasn't seen you in some time. You know the others."

"That's great, Dad."

Una Restaurante.

Uncle Jim was with Dad, We drove several blocks into Fort Lee. After abbraccio familiare (big hug) my uncle asked if I was hungry, a loaded question designed more to prepare for the meal rather than if I had eaten. I knew the drill. "I haven't eaten since breakfast."

My father called the restaurant a week earlier making reservations for a party of eight. "Well, then, I guess you won't be disappointed," he said, smiling, as he parked the car. The restaurant, Irk's, was Italian, translation: sauce, pasta and a full menu, served country style, from family recipes and wines from the old country. "Bring an appetite and loosen your belt!" This was a serious eating establishment.

At the entrance a small bar greeted customers. Hats and coats were accepted by the waiter. Rosario, the owner, met us at the door, addressing each of us by name, except me. As Jack's son, I was Il Doctore, accepted as family. The waiter took our coats and seated us. I recalled Irk's, a small restaurant in a quiet neighborhood offering "la cena", a formal dinner, with the freshest vegetables grown and meats raised in southern Italy, flown to New York and served at banquets (banchetti private), in a formal meal for special occasions. To the cognoscenti along the Hudson River, it was the "best food in town".

Dress code was business suit, tie and starched shirt, box white. A small dining room accommodated guests at a long banquet table. Five small round tables were placed away from the table. A photo of Mouseketeer Annette Funicello, in her mid-thirties hung above table in the corner. Four tuxedoed waiters wearing white aprons attended us ensuring privacy. If a nosey diner happened to overhear conversation of local patrons, it might be "sfortunato" (unfortunate) for him.

The music of halcyon days in the 1950's flowed through speakers, "American Bandstand" and "Your Hit Parade" filled the air. Dean Martin, of "Mambo Italiano", Connie Francis with "Who's Sorry Now", and crooner, Perry Como. "Old blue eyes", Frankie Sinatra, and Mario Lanza, "America's answer to Caruso". Singers from all over frequented adding notoriety to the place; Frankie Laine with "Jezebel" and "That's

My Desire", wailing Louis Prima's rock and roll too, had customers singing between the courses. The music set the mood and diners loved it. It was the place to meet, eat and enjoy life.

The Diners

As each guest was seated, he was offered a tray of aperitivi. Uncle Jim was of average height, a bit portly with an easy smile. He owned a demolition and transport company in South Orange specializing in disassembling historical homes, stone by stone, brick by brick. He transported them hundreds of miles to be reassembled in another state on beautiful, landscaped, estates. Some dated from colonial times. He was a good-natured man with a sense of humor who lived in Rutherford.

In 1942 he was drafted into the US army, and stationed at Army Air Force Base, 15th Headquarters in Tunis, Tunisia. Because he spoke Italian, he was assigned to communications, participating in the six-month Battle of Anzio in Italy during the winter and spring of 1944. He was skilled at laying wire and and was ordered to run communications to forward combat units during the battle. He was acrophobic and told his captain of his fear of heights. The captain's response was succinct and direct. He quietly responded; the assignment was critical, dangerous, and he risked being shot by a sniper. Unfortunately, if he disobeyed the order, the outcome might be the same and he could also be shot. So...he better work fast because the more time exposed stringing wire in the open, on poles, the greater the risk of getting shot, and there were a lot of poles. He was issued a Thompson submachinegun and counseled, "Don't worry about the height of the poles, sergeant, not getting shot is more of a priority."

The Germans retreated to Monte Casino, an ancient monastery south of Rome. The battle lasted six months with continuous Allied bombings. Enormous human casualties, 51,000 Allied, 27,000 German and Italian, and 37,000 non-combatants. The monastery was completely destroyed with its library containing irreplaceable religious manuscripts and paintings. Throughout the conflict Uncle Jim maintained open communications between Allied combat units, caught malaria and received the Bronze Star for meritorious conduct in combat. He sent a snapshot to Dad, crouched by a pole, cradling his tommy gun. Dad gave me the picture and told me the story. It was amazing. But for the rest of his life, he never climbed steps more than one at a time without holding onto a handrail or someone's arm.

Lou Zola was an affable, educated and experienced thirty-year-old, master mechanic, with abundant knowledge of cars, maintenance manuals on American and foreign makes. He took pride knowing the differences in models, engines, hydraulic brakes and power steering units. Dad often his advice and never argued with his judgment. A chain smoker, unfortunately, he died young from lung cancer before he was fifty. I saw him toward the end. He came to thank Dad for all he had done for him. He was thin and held my father's arm as he coughed. I did not attend his funeral, but my brother did and told me that Dad was quiet for a week afterward.

Bill Krause, a friend of Lou Zola, and Rutherford Chief of Police wore street clothes to the restaurant. He was born and raised in Rutherford, graduated from Farleigh Dickenson University a few blocks from his home and then the New Jersey State Police Academy. He rose in rank through merit, leadership, and good judgement to become highly respected in Bergen County law enforcement. He maintained a rapport with county residents, some with dubious reputations. He knew them all. Fort Lee was also home to certain underworld characters and fugitives from New York. Because of this, he never visited the Jersey side of the Hudson River from Alpine to Newark, unarmed. A slight bulge was visible on his waste beneath his suit coat.

Bill Claffey was a veteran, having seen action in the Pacific during WW II, "island hopping" toward Tokyo. He played craps and always had "folding money" in his pocket. A salesman for a company that sold steel tubing to refurbish boilers, he found summer jobs helping me save money for my return to college each fall. My job was to carry old, rusted tubes away and carry new tubes for welders to replace them retubing high pressure commercial boilers. This employment helped me decide my future. Carrying a six-foot long three-inch diameter steel tubes up two flights of stairs on my shoulders and returning with filthy used ones all day, as a career, was a distant second choice when compared to medicine.

Frank Pistilli was diminutive seventy-year-old plumber and friend of my father from the 1930s. I met him as a boy. Born Sicily, from Messina, small in stature with dark skin and deep-set Arabic eyes. He spoke short sentences and punctuated in Sicilian dialect, some of which my father refused to translate for me. He was gentle despite his physical appearance, a skilled "jack of all trades", offering to help friends when needed, muscle to move furniture, skill to build a new chimney, lay flagstone for a patio, remove trash and rubble. He would come at any hour to fix a broken pipe. It was rumored that he had "connections".

On Chestnut Street and Union Avenue Dad ran a filling station. Walter Edwards, a house painter, had a shop there too. He was meticulous man, attending to details of his work and his person. He wore a dark three-piece pin stripped suit to Irk's, nodding to the group when welcomed by my father. Years ago my father hired him to paint our Tudor home of wood and stucco. One morning as my father and watched him again unloading ladders from his truck at ten 10:45AM, he said, "You know son, that man is never going to die from over-work." And another time, "You know, he does good work. Not much, but what he does is good." Dad had a sense of humor. When Walter finished, Dad paid him.

Howie Schwartz owned a secondhand appliance and repair shop around the corner. He loved Italian food and was delighted to accept the invitation to come. A small stout man from Poland who spoke English with a heavy Polish accent, he had run from the Nazis, first to Canada and then to New Jersey many years ago. His shop was filled with out-of-date housewares, lamps, fireplace andirons and the like. If a housewife or repairman needed a broken appliance repaired or replaced, a radio or toaster part, Howie, would say, "I have one." or "I can get it for you wholesale."

He said this so often that his friends gave him the nickname, "I can get it for you, wholesale, Howie."

If we needed a special fuse, connecter, secondhand Mixmaster, anything, my father told me, "Go over and ask, 'I can get it for you, Howie', first."

Funny, but he usually had it or knew where to get it.

Dinner

Walter quietly took his seat and buttoned his dinner napkin to his shirt, to prevent the odd drop of sauce staining it. The rest of the diners sat down and tucked their linen napkins beneath their collars. Like soldiers in foxholes agog, they waited. Rosario lowered the music as the aperitivo, pouring a medium bodied red Sicilian wine, Nero D'Avola, from the lava slopes of Mt. Etna. Finger food followed: Parma prosciutto, fichi freschi, olive marinate, terrina d'anatra (duck terrine), fresh radishes, stuffed chilies and carciofi marinate e gresini still warm .

A simple wedding soup followed. The name reflects the marriage of small pork and beef meatballs with onion, a little fresh bread, garlic beaten egg parmesan mix, boiled, in chicken broth with escarole until the marriage is consummated. Eyes rolled as soup and white carricante wine teased the palate.

Table conversation increased, empty cups were cleared and the Primi Piatti, descended. Fresh sardines, from Sicily, cleaned and boned, with thinly sliced small bulb finocchio mated with fresh perciatelli, melded with zafferano (saffron), and completed with ribes essiccato (dried currants), A labor of love offered by Franco, Rosario's cousin. This was Pasta con le Sarde, the national dish of Sicily, from his mother, Nanna Terragrossa's, recipe, served with hard crusted Sicilian bread, fresh from the oven and white Piccolo Fiore, native Sicilian wine, simple and dry.

"This is quite a meal", I whispered to my father."

"Shhh..." He smiled. "Pace yourself. You have a long way to go," as the table talk around them increased.

The plates were cleared the glasses were refilled with nero d'avola. Diners became friends, commenting on the courses. Howie spoke up and asked, "Oh, this is beautiful, Jack. How did you find this place?"

"It's easy, Howie. Dad replied with a smile, "and I can get it for you wholesale ..." Everyone laughed, including Howie.

My father smiled as Bill Krause's eyes caught his. The Chief of Police isn't always looking for crooks and in his mind, Jack, had found a good restaurant.

To cleanse the palate, a caprese salad was served. Beautiful slices of beefsteak tomatoes from the Agriculture Department Rutgers University at peak of ripeness and fresh imported mozzarella da bufala, finished with sweet basil, olive oil, salt and a red wine vinegar.

Now bearing down on the beguiled dinner guests came Il Secondo. A perfectly broiled veal chop sliced and stuffed with a small link of sweet Italian sausage.

Smiles and conversation filled the air as dishes were cleared and the Frutta e Dolce courses were placed on the table. Coarsely chopped fresh fruit, and sweet pastries now served before, cannoli, apples baked in Regaleali wine and sfince crème puffs.

A great dining experience, like a symphony, must conclude with a coda. Strong expresso coffee was served. Then a digestivo is offered, to those still able to partake. Amaro is a brandy-based herbal liqueur blended with herbs, flowers, roots, bark, citrus peel, and spices sweetened with sugar syrup and aged from a few months to a few years. Sipped from a small clear glass.

The Well-Dressed Gentleman

When the diners first arrived, two men were there seated at a corner table. They looked up as our group was seated and ignored us. One of them in a dark suit, slightly rumpled, was nursing a glass of wine. The other, rolling a toothpick in his mouth, wearing in a double-breasted pinstriped suit that also needed pressing, had a bulge beneath the left breast pocket,. A small plate of antipasti lay before them. They sat quietly, occasionally picking an olive from the plate. After a while, one stood up quietly and left through the kitchen. His companion stayed and picked at antipasti. Our group sat down and took no notice. I watched as the man lit a cigarette, glance over at us, and then make eye contact with the waiter. An uncomfortable feeling of being watched came over me.

The dinner continued with each course more delicious than the last. We were enjoying a traditional Italian dinner with Italian American spin, too much of everything. As the vitello stuffed with sweet sausage was served, a well-dressed man entered the restaurant. He wore fedora slightly cocked and a camel hair coat was draped over his shoulders. Rosario, saw him immediately, walked to him and took his hat and coat. He walked to the corner table. The seated man rose and sat down again. His clothes were impeccable, silk suit, white shirt box clean, and clean shaven, complete with wafting cologne, un gentiluomo.

After a few comments between the two men, he got up and approached our table. No one in the restaurant seemed to notice what was happening...but no one moved, either. "Hello Bill." he said, to the Chief of Police, in a deferential manner.

Bill Krause turned to him, his snub-nosed revolver bulging visibly from beneath his sport coat and answered, "Hello Charles."

"It's been a while since we've seen you here." The Charles responded.

"The food and wine are very good." Bill replied.

"I just wanted to say hello," and after a few platitudes he returned to the corner table.

An eerie feeling came over me and I whispered, "Bill, who is that guy?"

"He's mafia, currently under indictment in Newark for gambling and prostitution" he said nonchalantly.

"Can you arrest him or do anything?"

He said, "Charlie Fingers? He's OK so long as he stays out of my town, and he knows it. Besides, look around. Do you see any women here?"

I understood. Be prepared. His reference to women meant that if there was a confrontation, women would not be involved, a sort of honor among thieves. It was a men's night out for relaxation. Charlie Fingers returned to his seat and asked the waiter for an anisette. After several minutes, the pinstriped man returned and motioned to Charlie that his Cadillac was outside. Rosario brought him his hat and coat and bid goodnight. Charlie Fingers and nodded to Bill as he left.

The meal was outstanding, but I felt a little uncomfortable for the rest of the evening. The bulges beneath the topcoats of Charlie and his friend's jacket were not the work of a rumpled suit or a bad tailor. We finished dinner in style, with Cuban cigars, compliments of Rosario, who saw us to the door.

When we left, I asked Dad why he had chosen to eat there. And with a smile, he answered, "It's the safest place in town. No one knowingly wants to poke a stick into a hornet's nest."

Coda

I never returned to Irk's Cucina Italiana nor to Fort Lee for that matter. The restaurant is long gone as are the customers who talked of that great dinner. Charlie Fingers, the "gentiluomo elegante" with whom Bill Krause spoke that night was arrested some years later and sent to federal prison for reasons I don't recall. The gathering of men on a Wednesday night at Irk's gave me wonderful insight into the lives of those old friends and that banquet. There was a certain camaraderie among them as they bantered with each other. They all grew up in Bergen County bought the goods and used the services provided by people like themselves. They talked of things in life that mattered. I felt a warmth for the old timers and young men there who worked to provide for their families. There also was an odd lingering tolerance of the thugs, part of the underworld working in the shadows of New York. I did not know their names or what they did, and it was best that I didn't. But I still recall the discomfort of witnessing Bill Kraus' composure as he engaged Charlie Fingers and his thugs at our table. That bulge on his belt remained with me for years afterward whenever I thought about Irk's.

Dad and I drove home to Maywood. My mother was asleep, and we said good night to each other and abbracciato. I crawled into my childhood bed. The events of the evening became a blur. Later in life when I thought of Irk's and the magnificent dinner, the embellished tales from times long past would come alive. The vision of the men there, now gone many years returned and stirred those memories. If I told that story today, Dad would look at me and smile." ....Irk's? Ha! You mean, Irk's?", he would say ...

GIACOMO J. SAMMARCO as a child and teenager sang professionally in opera, and as a soloist with Columbus Boychoir. He attended Dartmouth College, Tulane University School of Medicine, Case Western Reserve University School of Medicine, served in the US Public Health Service, published numerous articles in orthopaedic journals, chapters in orthopaedic texts, and edited four books. He and his wife, Ruthann, (nee Busse), spend much of their time at their vacation home in Chautauqua, NY, where they participate in educational and entertainment presentations and enjoy their extended family throughout the seasons.

13

Le Baiser

HARRY SANTEN

Rodin carved *Le Baiser* ("The Kiss") in marble in 1882. A naked man and a naked woman embrace, their lips touching, or almost. His hand warms her hip. Her arm wraps gently around his neck. Does the carving portray affectionate love or perhaps the incidents of passion, or both?

The sculpture, larger than life, measures over six feet. Rodin submitted it to museums and galleries, but art critics rejected it as unfit for public viewing because of its "eroticism."

In a sculpture class where I was a student, we discussed his *John the Baptist* and his *Monument to Balzak*, then decided as a class we would like to work on copying *The Kiss*. Our teaching professor approved. He found a man and a woman who would model the sculpture naked. There was no eroticism involved. The models would affect requested poses while the students worked hard to sculpt accurately.

There were ten of us in the class working to become better sculptors. We were all amateurs, twenty-five to thirty years old. None of us had worked in marble, sculpting in clay because that material is pliable.

Work in the class progressed nicely. Feet and hands, both very difficult, were made and remade. Legs were modified to become more like the models. Bodies were slimmed to match the naked figures. We were like Picasso, modelling in clay. The professor went from person to person with individual advice. At the conclusion of each session we wrapped our unused clay and our own sculpture in plastic to keep it moist and pliable. All of the sculptures were much smaller than life size.

The two models reenacted the Rodin work holding the same pose, statue-like for thirty minutes. They then took a break, wrapping in terry cloth robes for rest and warmth. Modelling any pose is difficult enough

but the position of the two figures in *The Kiss* made it even more so.

After each class the models dressed quickly and left. The rest of us remained for camaraderie and criticism from the professor or just for the enjoyment of being together. Someone always brought a bottle or two of wine so there was closeness and a friendliness that developed.

After one sculpture session with the wine freely flowing, one of the women students said, "Because we are sculpting a kiss, wouldn't it be interesting and fun to talk about some of our own kissing experiences?"

Ordinarily such a question may have produced no answers, only silence. However, because we had been closely involved with *The Kiss* and because the wine lessened our temerity, I spoke up. "I have three kissing stories to tell," I said. "Each of them relates actual facts and the third one tells a key story of my life." The response was "Great, let's hear the stories."

The First Story

"At age fourteen I was invited to a house party for a weekend at a farm near Cincinnati for 20 boys and girls. Miss Mary, the aunt of one of the boys, had arranged the party for her nephew, Friday evening to Sunday noon. Today we all know that house parties, often romantic ones, were famous in numerous novels, but that extended well beyond the experience of any of us then as young teenagers.

"The boys and girls slept in separate dormitories. We saw this as a new, different and exciting experience. The first evening all of us went to a barbecue dinner where many of us met for the first time. We went to different schools and lived in different neighborhoods.

"That evening I met Sally, who much to my surprise and pleasure led to this story about my first kissing experience which occurred memorably on a hay ride the following evening.

"At the farm at dusk two hay wagons arrived, full to the top with hay, comfortable to sit or lie in. I climbed into one of the wagons along with four other boys and five girls. One of the girls was Sally. Although we had been introduced, we really didn't know one other, at least not yet.

"She had a comfortable presence about her, friendly, relaxed and happy with being there. She wore jeans and a wool western style shirt which to some extent hid a fine figure. She was a very attractive young woman.

"The conversation in the hay wagon was lively and continuous, then someone said "let's play temptation." Everyone knew the game: A boy and a girl get very close to one another, their faces and lips getting close and closer but their lips not touching, not kissing but just tempting. Actual kissing was considered against the rules, though rule- breaking was not unknown.

"Sally surprised me. She leaned over and said, 'lets you and I play the game and I'll go first.' I lay back in the hay with my face and lips up, ready to be tempted. Sally leaned over, her mouth and lips approaching. In the rules of the game she should have put her lips close to mine, then resisted the temptation.

"I didn't anticipate what would happen next. I had just turned 14 weeks before. I had never kissed a girl. I closed my eyes to increase the sense of the temptation when her lips touched mine. They didn't just touch. They remained there, soft and warm and slightly moving. My young heart beat a newly found rhythm.

"I was surprised, but so much more. I liked what was happening. I was content and more, warm and alive. How could I not like this first-ever kiss or ever remove it from my fondest of memories? That first kiss has retained its vibrancy over the years. I still feel two lips caressing and remaining, soft and warm and slightly moving.

At our next sculpting session, the figures were better. The wine flowed again and the professor asked, "Are you going to continue with the second story?"

The Second Story

I stood up, took a sip of wine and said, "Here it is: Two of my friends, Dave and Charlie, and I, all high school freshmen, were walking on a small private lane in a neighborhood where everyone knew one another. There we met and began to chat with three 'older girls' from the neighborhood—Tippy, Nancy and Pat. They were sophomores, a year ahead of us. After a not-lengthy conversation, the girls huddled and came back to us with a proposition: 'You boys are young, attractive and probably inexperienced. Would you like to learn how to kiss?' We didn't hesitate. How could we not agree?

"We were in front of Nancy's house where a station wagon was parked. Tippy climbed into the front seat, inviting Jack to join her. Nancy climbed into the back seat, inviting Charlie to join her. Pat got into the back rear seat, inviting me to join her.

"We really did, we took kissing lessons from three most attractive 'older women.' We switched partners so each of the boys had three lessons and the girls three partners. Amid smiles and laughter, the kisses were short and the techniques simple. "

The Third Story

"After another sculpting session, the wine again flowed as did my next story about an event which took place much later. Ann and I knew one another but were not close. We had met at a jug band party in Louisville, where Ann lived, and after some time had passed I was invited to return. This time Ann and I were attracted, bee to flower, one to the other, wondering if the pollen had predictions.

"Later we met in New York. We saw each other wherever and whenever we could. Ann learned my love for poetry and in person and in her numerous letters she often quoted one of the many poems she had memorized.

"One afternoon in the country together, we saw tiger lilies blooming on a hillside. They called to us, the call of ancient sirens. We heard the call. We wanted to be among the lilies. We wanted to enjoy their beauty and the path our own lives were taking.

"We were resting in the grass with the tiger lilies as a backdrop when I put my arm around Ann's shoulder, my hand resting on her hip. Our lips were touching, almost. I hugged her, then kissed her, long and lovingly saying, 'Ann, I love you' and she replied, 'I love you, too.'"

"I had not once in my life ever kissed a woman that I loved and had never loved a woman that I had kissed. This kiss was long like hyacinths blooming, but was there a commitment, a long-term commitment? The answer needed no expression after Ann said: "You gave my hyacinths first a year ago;

They called me the hyacinth girl.
Yet, when we came back, late, from the hyacinth garden,
Your arms full, and your hair wet, I could not
Speak and my eyes failed, I was neither
Living nor dead, and I knew nothing,
Looking into the heart of light, the silence."

"With the commitment, we got to know one another better, to be more together and to write more letters. Each togetherness enhanced our love and our desire to be together. We wanted to be like intertwining grape vines producing good fruit.

"Six months later Ann and I were alone at my parent's home, lying on the rug in the evening. I put my arms around Ann and said 'I love you, Ann. Will you marry me?' She looked deeply into my eyes replying with a definitive nod of her head and the simple word 'Yes.' My hand rested on her hip, our lips almost touching. Her arm rested gently around my neck.

"We kissed, sealing the future, a long-term love affair. I have kissed a woman that I loved and I love the woman I kissed."

HARRY H. SANTEN was born in 1929. He attended St. Xavier High School, Georgetown University and the U.C. College of Law. He has been named a Great Living Cincinnatian and has served as president of the Cincinnati Bar Association, Cincinnati Opera Association, Legal Aid Society, Volunteer Lawyers of the Poor Foundation and the Heart Association of Southwestern Ohio. He is a potter, a writer and a wine lover.

Poem Turning On The Word "Orange"

There were never enough flies.
Corpses lay unconsumed everywhere—
cattle by the freeway like stinking Volkswagens,
drifts of rotting mice outside all the barns,
lengths of copperheads crisp as bacon
draped over skillet-hot curbs.

Preachers called for flies from their pulpits,
politicians promised flies in every pot
along with the conventional chicken,
and boys in ballcaps on smoky clanging corners
dealt black market maggots
in slimy plastic baggies.
All was decay and stench and silence and then

Orange deliverance came,
morning orange as a creamsicle,
sweet-smelling as a honeycomb.
Great crevices opened in high school football fields
in Hazard and Pittsburgh and Newport,
and a billion flies emerged,
their collective hum as loud as the Goodyear blimp.
Bluebottles and deerflies and horseflies
descended like quivering rain
on everything, everywhere,
and all carrion disappeared,
and even morticians and hard-up poets
and the owners of small groceries
hugged one another
and sang out to each other
in buzzing flying sonnets.

– RICHARD HAGUE

14

WHOSE KNEES?

RANDOLPH L. WADSWORTH JR.

Faceplant

It was around eight o'clock on a Saturday morning about forty years ago. Early October, about forty-five degrees, mist rising, heavy dew. As I was walking the dog back to the barn, a nondescript mass in front of Sallie's beehive twenty yards to the left caught my eye. I trotted over for a closer look. The dog hung back. Otherwise fearless, he was wary of the hive.

The mass was a heap of dead bees, ashen gray and sodden with dew.

Allowing just time for the dog to justify his walk, I rushed back to rouse Sallie with the scary news.

I shook her gently awake and told her what I had seen. Her only reaction was to ask if the coffee was ready. Since Sallie used to say she didn't know her name till after the first shot, that didn't surprise me; but I was taken aback when she then asked me to fill her mug and lay on an English muffin with some of that Dundee marmalade, if there was any left.

When Sallie arrived in the dining room, I asked why she was so unconcerned by the slaughter at the hive. She said it was probably to be expected; in which case we might as well take our time. If she was wrong, better to eat than to tackle an emergency on an empty stomach. The dead bees were beyond caring, and what the live ones in the hive didn't

126

know wouldn't hurt them. The woman could be infuriatingly rational.

At the hive, Sallie knelt to examine the carnage. Rising, she turned to me and said, "It's just the drones, you silly goose."

I thought of saying she had the wrong fowl but forbore in favor of a dope slap. I had forgotten that drones, whose only job is to mate with virgin queens, are of no use in winter and are driven from the hive to prevent needless consumption of the colony's resources. Clearly, this lot had been turned out overnight and left to die of hunger and exposure. For me not to have twigged was an embarrassing lapse. At least next year I'd know better.

Chastened, I helped Sallie open the hive for a quick survey, a chore that required more lifting than she could manage on her own. The workers were as busy as—well, bees—raising the brood that would see the colony through the winter.

After we had closed the hive, Sallie gave me a peck on the cheek, thanked me for my help, and suggested that before the next spring I might revisit her beekeeper's manual. You may be sure I did.

But how did we come to be keeping bees at all?

The Venture's Origin

We had been living for several years in an 1883 farmhouse on six acres just north of the main road between Brookville, Indiana, and Oxford, Ohio, where I was teaching English literature at Miami University. A mile west of the state line, we were eight miles from each of the towns.

One morning several months before my faux pas with the drones, Sallie surprised me at breakfast with the news that someone she had met on a trip had put bees in her bonnet. Knowing that she liked honey, this person remarked that our place was ideal for a hive or two, surrounded as we are by ample forage. And there was more: at work I parked just a few yards from the modest brick cottage that from 1859 to 1887 housed the family of the Reverend L. L. Langstroth, billed by the site's historical marker as "The Father of American Beekeeping."

Sallie liked the idea of harvesting enough honey to give away to selected friends, with a bit left over for us. Equally, she liked the overlap with Langstroth, which seemed somehow appropriate, almost a sign or invitation. Moreover, she had done some homework and had arranged to attend a demonstration by a distributor of beekeeping equipment a few miles east in Monroe, Ohio. She hoped I would join her, adding that she could keep bees only if I agreed to help around the edges.

Three minutes into the distributor's demo, I realized why Sallie would need a partner: she did not feel competent to assemble a hive and its fiddly paraphernalia; and there would be more lifting than a woman five foot three could handle alone: a hive box full of comb and honey can weigh over sixty pounds.

We left Monroe with a complete starter kit: material to assemble into a three-box hive; two beekeeper's suits; and a tin pot with squeeze bellows and a spout called a "smoker". (This because for some unknown reason smoke calms bees.) We had as well an order for starter bees, complete with a fertile queen, to be settled when the hive was ready.

I set to work at once on the hive, which took the better part of two days. The three boxes were easy. Putting together thirty frames to hold comb was a task I swore never to repeat: the small surcharge for ready-made was a luxury I'd be happy to pay going forward.

The hive being ready, we gave the all-clear for the starter bees to be dispatched. A few days later, while Sallie was at a meeting thirty or more miles away in Indian Hill, the Brookville Post Office called to say they had a batch of bees that our Rural Route driver was not about to put in her car; so of course I had to fetch them. They were in a cubical box, screened on its sides with wood on its top, bottom, and ends. There were two enclosures inside, the larger packed with worker bees, the smaller with the queen.

When Sallie got home, we saw them into the hive and crossed our fingers. The following morning, warned not to disturb the newcomers, we left them to their own devices.

By afternoon, the place was humming with groups of workers behaving rather oddly. After walking a foot or two up the side of the hive, they launched themselves backwards. They would then hover back and forth facing the hive in larger and larger arcs until they were out of sight. There was also a succession of bees returning to the hive at similar intervals and landing at the entrance, where some lingered, some went inside right away, and some crawled up the hive and took another turn. Finally, so many bees were involved that they began to overlap, and we feared they might be preparing to swarm. But the numbers declined gradually until, after a few solitary stragglers, there were none. This was our first experience of orientation flights, which are nothing more than what the term suggests.

Bees do not instinctively know where they live. They must memorize the hive's location in relation to distinctive landmarks so they can find their way home. Some take longer than others, which could explain the repeated flights. And some might need encouragement, resulting in crowds led by experienced foragers. These flights show that the hive is consistently producing foragers to keep it supplied with nectar, pollen, and water.

The Right Word

Home for all but two weeks of that summer, we noticed a consistent increase in our colony's population, a good sign.

Only one episode between the arrival of our bees and my faceplant with the drones sticks in my memory.

The Big Red Hornet

Several weeks after our bees had settled in, I was mowing the spacious lawn in front of the hive. It was about three in the afternoon, hazy, temperature in the low eighties, no wind. On about the fourth pass, directly in front of the hive and about twenty feet from it, I heard bees around my head. The mower, a red sixty-inch Yazoo, was audible at a quarter mile; so I had to assume that any bees I could hear above its snarl were numerous and royally pissed off. I hit the kill switch and hit the deck, face down, hands under me, sun helmet tipped back over my neck. Luckily, I was wearing a long-sleeved shirt to keep the sun off my arms.

Met with silence, I got up and hoofed it to the house, fearing the return of larger forces. I found Sallie in the library and told her what had happened. We were both puzzled. The bees had experienced the mower several times by now, but only in the cool of early evening. I was mowing early on this day because we had been invited to supper with friends in Oxford. It must have been the hour that set them off.

Wondering what the bees might do next, we went to the door of our laundry room, which looks north onto the bees' lawn. Almost at once a large horde emerged from the hive and began to assault the mower in a cycle of waves. They did not dash themselves against the monster as if to sting, but swooped in and away from different angles, as if to harry it and drive it off. This was material for relief on two counts: the population of the colony was clearly growing at a good rate, and the attacking bees were not harming themselves in the exercise. We were still puzzled, though, by the sudden violent aversion to the mower, so we continued to watch.

After only another minute or two, the bees returned to the hive, apparently assured that the mower, now silent, was no longer a threat.

Within another two minutes we saw a goodly number begin an orientation flight; and almost immediately following that, a much larger squadron headed northwest without looking back, obviously on a foraging run. The mowing had interfered with not one, but two, important operations. Rule underlined: the best times to mow around a honeybee hive are just after sunrise and just before sunset, when bees are least active. They don't like to be distracted when they're learning or working. I respected their wishes for the rest of the mowing season.

Following the advice we'd been given, we did not harvest any honey; and, just after the eviction of the drones, we buttoned up the hive for winter. Because opening a hive in winter disturbs the clustering of the bees that keeps them warm, we left it closed until the bees began their normal pattern of flights in late spring. Our next adventure was just around the corner.

Swarm

Swarming of honeybees in late spring is normal in healthy hives. Keepers who are prepared to capture a swarm before it moves off can add a colony to their stock. By the time our bees had made it through their first winter, we were prepared. We had new hive supplies on hand, and we had both read up on how to trap a swarm.

Immediately behind our farmhouse, there is a waist-high standpipe with a hose bib. Around noon one late spring day, I noticed that the pipe had grown as stout as a fire hydrant. It was covered with bees, which must have swarmed from our hive, not a hundred feet away. As with the starter bees, Sallie was away at a meeting. Waiting for her return would risk the departure of the swarm, so the would-be capture was up to me.

The instructions called for a white bed sheet; a long, soft-bristled brush; the smoker, and a container for the bees. I had ready a plastic garbage can, its top drilled with breathing holes. There was one hitch. Sallie didn't like white sheets. The closest I could find was pale yellow with printed flowers. Whatever.

The trick was to put the sheet at the base of the bees' perch and place the garbage can about four feet away with its mouth facing the swarm. Then I was to brush bees onto the sheet. With luck, they might mistake the receptacle for a hollow log suitable as a nesting site.

I lit the smoker, gave the bees a few puffs and began brushing. When a goodly number were on the sheet, they began to amble toward the would-be log but stopped about halfway. I held my breath and kept brushing. Before long, at what I now surmise was a signal from the queen, there was a mad rush for the for the dark opening.

I'll interrupt here for a moment to say I later learned that the signal was a pheromone, a smell emitted from an organism to elicit a specific response from other members of its species. (Think of a bitch in heat.) But I digress.

I moved the bees into the shade, plopped Sallie's bee suit next to them, and began to put together the new hive. I had nearly finished when the Head Keeper arrived at about five-thirty. Taking the hint, she came running to my workplace behind the house, dragging her bee suit and undoing her skirt.

"More! More!" I cried.

"That's not funny," she snapped. "We have work to do."

"I'm getting there," I said. "I'll be done as soon as you suit up and put some more chips in the smoker."

A good half hour later we lugged the new hive bodies and their frames to the spot I had prepared next to the original hive. We put the sheet in front of their new home and opened the trash can. To our relief, the queen trotted out and led the workers right in.

Newly out of hive makings, we hustled over to Monroe to stock up. And a good thing, too. Not two weeks later, early in the afternoon, a phone call from a neighbor alerted me to a swarm of bees. The caller was Constance, a colleague who taught creative writing. She and her husband, Frank, a freelance writer, lived about a mile away on a southeast beeline, a mile and a quarter by county roads on a north-south grid.

Breathless, Constance told me she had been musing on her south-facing veranda while Frank was writing or maybe napping upstairs when she thought she must be seeing things because out of nowhere there was what looked like a scaled-down murmuration—and wasn't that a wonderful word?—of starlings like what we see out here in the fall but it was bees not starlings and they had swooped and darted in front of her for a few seconds and were now clustered on a fence post just west of the house and remembering that Sallie and I kept bees she wondered if I might be able to deal with them.

Whew!

When she finally paused for a breath, I said I'd try. Success would yield us a third colony; failure would at least drive the bees away from their place.

Twenty minutes saw me suited up and at the fencepost. Another fifteen saw the bees housed in the green garbage can and the couple, who had watched from a window, suitably impressed. I say "suitably" because I had said nothing about the usual docility of swarming bees and shamelessly planned to leave our friends free to tout my exploit as if it had involved uncommon courage and a mastery of technique. A few "aw, shucks" moments later, I was preparing to load up when a single bee appeared, doubtless a returning scout. Following a few seconds of confusion, it lit atop the garbage can, where I had left the bee brush. I reflexively picked up the brush and gently persuaded the bee into the palm of my left hand, where it was content to rest long enough for me to drop the brush, lift the lid, and drop it in. I was compelled to explain why what I had done was neither dangerous nor difficult. Filled with honey for a trip, swarming bees are notably laid back.

When Sallie got home, we persuaded the bees into their new home and went to Oxford for supper, where Sallie told several colleagues and friends the story of both my swarm exploits, generously acknowledging my progress as a partner in her enterprise. Not a little pleased with myself, I thought I was the bee's knees.

I'll let that pass for now and turn to the bees left in our original hive by our swarm.

The Remnant

Ordinarily, when honeybees swarm, between half and two-thirds of the workers leave with the queen. (If all the bees leave, they are said to have absconded.) Once we had hived our swarm, we looked into the first hive, where, to our relief, there were still quite a few bees. They would have selected a new queen, whose first order of business—if she had not yet done so—would be to mate.

To do that, she would first have to find a nearby drone congregation area, known as a DCA. The DCA is an upward-pointing aerial cone about 300 feet across at its base and between fifty and a hundred feet above the ground. It is usually found in an open space sheltered from the wind and marked by some notable visual feature. It will always be at a point where habitual bee flyways intersect, although not all such intersections yield DCAs. A DCA can last in place as long as local conditions remain stable. (There is one in southern England that has been in service for over two hundred years.) Nor is there ever a shortage of DCAs in an area with honeybees.

Exactly how drones find DCAs is not known, even though the question has been the subject of several ingenious studies; but find them they do.

And, since drones are known not to accompany swarms of any kind, we may be sure that our new queen would have been left with drones to help her find a DCA.

Weather permitting, drones make several flights a day. Fueled by only enough honey to sustain around twenty minutes of flight, they must make exquisite adjustments while aloft. (Think of an airplane pilot and the point of no return.) Ones that don't make it home or find another hive will starve. But that's their problem. Back to our queen and the scenario for mating.

A virgin queen begins her first nuptial flight just behind a flight of drones, guided by their pheromones.

Once she stumbles on a DCA, she flies to the very top of it and waits. Her own powerful queen pheromone attracts a host of drones formed into a comet configuration, led by the fastest and thus most fit in the group. The first to catch up to the virgin initiates a succession of aerial couplings—typically between ten and twenty—that will occur on this flight. This episode is only the prelude to a succession of flights that will leave her with between fifty and seventy million sperm cells collected in as many as fifty or more matings, likely in more than one DCA. A queen might lay up to two thousand eggs a day and as many as two hundred thousand eggs in her lifetime. For that she needs a lot of sperm.

And what of the drone who was first in line? Well, he won't be bragging to his buddies about how he scored with that hot queen. Thrown violently backward by the force of his ejaculation, he will fall away, only to find that his barbed endophallus, locked in the vaginal orifice of the queen, has remained in place, keeping half his abdomen with it. He may be dead before he hits the ground, but not before the next in line has removed his member, its barbs grown slack, and gone to work. Welcome once again to the dystopian life of the drone.

Since they were carrying on with orientation flights and foraging expeditions, our remaining bees clearly had satisfied the queen requirement. The current generation of workers, daughters of the queen that swarmed, were sisters to the workers next door. DCAs being the melting pots they are, the progeny of the new queen would have a different genome. Biodiversity is a Good Thing.

But what about the captured swarm in our second hive? Did the first to venture out recognize their surroundings? Or did they reorient as from scratch? Orientation flights and foraging continued, but a few flew back to the original hive before realizing their mistake and took off again. Within a handful of days, there were no bees flying to the old hive. Apparently, the majority caught on quickly, and only a few were slow learners. An enviable ratio, that.

It's now time to turn briefly to Lorenzo Lorraine Langstroth and his invention, both of which are far more worthy than I am to be called the bee's knees, an accolade that since the nineteen twenties implies excellence in a person, action, or object.

More on Langstroth

In addition to calling Langstroth the "Father of American Beekeeping," the historical marker at his cottage asserts that "... he discovered 'bee space,' an open space of not more than three-eighths of an inch which bees would not fill to bond their combs to hives. From this came the world's first moveable frame beehive, patented in 1852, which revolutionized beekeeping and the honey industry."

Issues of priority in the exploitation of bee space and in the construction of hives with movable frames are too complicated to go into here. Suffice it to say that Langstroth sought and acknowledged the help of Samuel Wagner, founder and first editor of the American Bee Journal. Wagner made him acquainted with the work of several European apiarists who also had invented hives with movable frames. Langstroth's innovation was a hive that was easier to manipulate and cheaper to make than any earlier design he was aware of. In 1852 he secured a patent that proved all-too easy for crafty imitators to clone with minor changes that let them escape royalties. Fighting the copiers took more time and money than Langstroth could muster, and he gave up trying. To help him, in 1859, his brother-in-law bought the cottage in Oxford, where Langstroth was able to continue his study of bee behavior and raise queens to sell. In the meantime, in 1853, Langstroth had written *Langstroth On The Hive And Honeybee*, in which he ruefully explains that he has turned to beekeeping because he has been "debarred by the state of his health from the more appropriate duties of his office."

Lorenzo Lorraine Langstroth was born on Christmas Day, 1810, in Philadelphia. In 1831 he took his degree in theology from Yale Divinity School, where he remained as a tutor for two more years. In 1836, he became Pastor of the Second Congregational Church (locally known as Old South Church) in Andover, Massachusetts. Subsequently, he spent time in and around Greenfield, Massachusetts, as minister and as a teacher in a school for young ladies. The state of health that drove him from preaching and teaching was what today we would think of as bouts of crippling depression. He could only be happy in an occupation that let him spend much time outdoors. A chance exposure to honeycomb led him to beekeeping, which would be his calling from then on. In the end, although he lost the battle with those who had infringed his patent, he won the war: variations on the Langstroth hive account for the vast majority of hives the world around.

At the time we were keeping bees, Sallie and I knew nothing of Langstroth but what's on the historical marker. I now realize that his path and ours to Oxford exhibit a correspondence that Sallie would have found uncannily prescient. As a student at Andover, I had attended service in the South Church; and the two of us had spent two years at the Northfield Schools, nine miles from Greenfield. I wonder.

Meanwhile, back at the farm, it was time for our first harvest.

First Harvest

Harvesting honey requires two judgment calls. In our latitude it's wise to leave an average healthy colony at least eighty pounds of honey for the winter, calculated at five to six pounds per frame. By the same token, no frame is considered ready for harvest or for winter use until nearly all the cells in its comb have been capped with beeswax. Thinking that we should regard both our remnant bees and the third lot as first-year colonies, we planned to take honey only from our bees that had swarmed.

One day, I think it was about the middle of September, a routine inspection of the middle hive showed that both conditions had been met. There was at least a hundred pounds of honey in the top two boxes of that hive, so we could safely take four frames.

We were set up to extract the honey on the porch at the northwest corner of the house, which features screen on the north and west, brick on the south, and wide sliding glass doors on the east that lead to our kitchen at the south end and a large pantry at the other. It was a good place for the job, allowing us to keep the mess out of the kitchen and to work away from any interference by the bees.

The first step was to cut or scrape the wax caps off the combs, a messy operation. We cut, using a heated knife.

We had bought, used, a hand-cranked centrifugal extractor on a stand high enough for a bucket to rest under its large spigot. It held two brackets, disposed across from each other and designed to hold the ten-inch frames from our hives. The honey, slung out of the comb and onto the wall of the extractor, oozes its way to the sloping bottom and to the spigot. Then it is filtered into a bucket through cheesecloth to strain out the larger bits of wax or comb. With this minimal treatment, the resulting product may be classed as "raw" honey.

Since the bees fill comb on both sides of each frame, our four frames required eight runs. I was tired of cranking long before the job was done.

Once the honey started to flow, bees began to collect on the screen. There were eventually so many that their buzzing drowned out the considerable racket from the extractor. I remarked to Sallie that they might regard what we called harvesting as theft. She thought it was more a question of their simply smelling something sweet and wanting to feast on it. In either case, we were operating ethically, leaving the bees plenty of honey for the winter. And besides, there was still goldenrod available for them to make new honey in the frames we had emptied. Even so, there was a lot of buzzing around the porch for three or four days. I wonder still.

When we had gotten the honey into a selection of Mason jars, we finally made two slices of toast and tried some. About halfway to molasses in both color and sweetness, it had an aftertaste we both found a little bitter, but only enough to add interest rather than to detract from an overall impression of richness. Sallie said she was not surprised, as her reading had warned that goldenrod could impart just such an effect. All the honey we were to harvest over the next several years would exhibit that piquant aftertaste, while the overall strength varied a little, depending on a myriad of other influences that inevitably change from year to year.

I have one more episode to recount. It was by far the scariest I can recall.

The Scariest Episode

In the downstairs bathroom of our farmhouse is a handsome embossed print on Japanese paper of honeybees in flight, their pollen baskets flecked with gold. I shudder every time I see it. It was a gift from Karen, a former graduate student of mine who had become a friend to both of us. When she asked if she could help us harvest our crop one year, we were happy to oblige. We had a spare bee suit, and help was always welcome.

On the appointed day, knowing supper would be late if we started at our usual late afternoon hour, Sallie prepared a cold collation.

Things went smoothly enough. As always, a few bees made their way onto the screened porch with the frames. Karen mostly just watched; but a couple of times she took off her gloves to help with the cheesecloth while I ferried frames, shortening the wait for supper. Even so, it was close to eight before we hit the table.

Sallie had prepared a chicken salad, and Karen had brought a Swiss Rosé that, lightly chilled, proved to be an excellent choice. While we were enjoying dessert and an espresso, Karen let slip that, when she was ten, a single bee sting had sent her to an emergency ward in anaphylactic shock, glibly adding that she had Epinephrine in the car, so, no problem. Somewhat acerbically, I said that we kept Epinephrine on hand, as well, and had been trained to inject it, but that we did not appreciate her making its need more likely. Had we known her history, we'd have asked her to watch from the kitchen through the sliding glass door.

Karen mumbled a brief apology. Then she disappeared for a moment and returned with a mailing tube, from which she drew that print of honeybees.

That harvest, our fourth, would be our last. Not long after, we gave away our bees and all our equipment to a local beekeeper. A change in our lives meant we would be spending the entire summer away in Canada at the resort that my extended family still own and operate.

Coda

Sallie died in 2017, eight days before our sixtieth anniversary. Whenever I recall our years of keeping bees, the aftereffect is like that of our honey: in flavor, not so much bitter as piquant; in memory, not so much bitter as poignant; the sweetness not compromised but complemented.

Born in 1935, **RANDOLPH L. WADSWORTH JR.** was brought up in Fort Thomas. My formal education concluded with two years at Andover, a B. A. from Princeton and a Ph.D. from Stanford. I taught English at Miami University from 1970 to 1988 and coached Miami's Rowing Club from then until 2016. I am now retired and living in Covington.

15

Musings on
Getting OLD

RICHARD G. WENDEL

I am not complaining about getting old as everyone repeatedly reminds me that the alternative is worse. But as an old friend recently commented, "growing old is not for sissies." I am 87; looking back it seems that time has passed quickly. This essay is meant to be insightful about the art of growing old graciously for this is a challenging achievement in this most transformative period of change in life's journey.

One indicator of becoming elderly is that reading the death notices and obituaries becomes a daily ritual, and you attend more memorial church services than regular Sunday religious services. Casual discussion between old men at the bridge table usually includes a focus on medical conditions and health concerns. As a licensed retired physician, I am looked to for more reliable comment and advice.

Old men and women are justifiably neurotic about their health. The most common medical condition discussed usually centers on the musculoskeletal system because degenerative arthritis is almost universal, and many have had joint replacements and physical therapy for one reason or another. Bragging or complaining about the PSA and cholesterol values rise to the top along with disabling disorders suffered by friends or family members. Often, due to an unpleasant experience, specific healthcare providers or hospital systems are trashed by one or more of the bridge players. Because older individuals generally go to see a menu of specialists and not just their Primary Care Physician, there are many medical encounters upon which to ruminate and make value judgments. Sometime there is a competition to see who can tell the most harrowing experiences they had with the healthcare system or express amazement at hospital bills that defy the accounting principles of Activity Based Costing.

A common problem that old folks often voice is the fact that their physicians are often on the cusp of retirement or recently retired. Switching doctors is not a seamless transaction. The hassle of delays in getting an appointment with a new doctor and the redundant paperwork is irksome. Moreover, your new doctors often are a part of a large multi-specialty group with many office locations that may frustrate your wanting to be seen by a single provider. And how do you put your trust in a host of new young doctors who look more like your grandson than the fatherly figures you're accustomed to?

The process of aging creeps up at a snail's pace and brings with it a decline in all systems for which you can easily compensate ...until the physiological reserves are exhausted. In sports, you must choose competition that matches your residual abilities to make a go of it. Unfortunately, the downward trajectory continues until you arrive at the last rung of the ladder and your more capable teammates diplomatically exclude you from the roster. Of course, before that time occurs other maladies may kick in such as irksome back pain, wonky knees and atrial fibrillation that render you physically incapable and in need of self- deselection. But being a sidelined spectator to a club tennis match and being familiar with your friend's tennis weapons is not a bad gig; especially when you can enjoy a beverage and make value judgments without the thrill of victory or the agony of defeat.

Limitations are the name of the game when you are old. But the body has remarkable physiological reserves, For instance, you can live normally on the function of one-quarter of one kidney and just half of one lung. You generally do not experience shortness of breath with regular activities until your Spirometry calculated one second Forced Expiratory Volume (FEV) is less than 70 percent (normal range being 80% to 120%.)

In the aging process, each of your body's 100 trillion cells age together in synchrony and reach the Hayflick Number of 40-60 cell division or mitosis before they become "senescent." This generalized progression correlates with your physiologic reserves. True, some friends die prematurely due to cancer, cardiovascular disease, accidents and so on. But those lucky ones that survive into their late seventies and beyond generally hit, what I call, the 'mortality wall' and experience what we, as medical residents, used to call a case of the 'dwindles.' My experience suggests that cognitive and mental faculties are more durable in old age than physical ones. Moreover, those individuals that reach 100 are usually thin, female and live a life of moderation in all things.

When you get old your circle or network of friends and acquaintances shrinks for multiple reasons. Some friends pass away; many migrate to be with their offspring in distant cities; some downsize and go into retirement communities; a few will experience progressive dementia, and sport groups dissolve because members develop physical issues. Also, retirement from gainful employment separates you from your co-worker friends and professional activities. Your offspring may fill some of the gaps, but they are often fully engaged in busy careers that may limit their time to visit and attend to your social needs.

Moreover, aging muffles your emotional energy and motivation to make new friends. You have little need to "social climb" and the repetition of having "been there and done that" often curtails enthusiasm. New adventures are not as appealing as staying home in a stress-free mode of routine that enables you to live within your comfort zone and physical restraints. This shrinkage of your social life, networking and striving to be connected occurs slowly but inexorably for most. The phenomena of "network collapse" is attested to by the fact that if you die young, the church pews are filled at your memorial service, but if you die old, only primary family members attend unless you are a public or prominent figure.

For individuals who had dynamic and fruitful careers that brought with it the power of position and influence, the slope of decline into old age is more transformational. Your mate is generally not willing to assume the role of an employee or "go-fer". He or she may enjoy more time together every day but not necessarily for lunch. You no longer have associates or employees that defer to your judgment and heed your instructions. In reality, the command-and-control equation is partially reversed. Your family and young associates are equals in the hierarchy of things and often must be consulted and cajoled to do your bidding.

You are forced to relinquish some control; that is, unless you own all the stock in the company, retain your ceremonial position as Chairman of the Board, or have significant retirement assets that focus the interest of your offspring and charities.

Stated differently, if you are a professional, an upper-level manager, a successful businessperson, a CEO, or master craftsman, you usually must transform from being the independent style leader to relying more on your 'soft-power' social skills to satisfy your narcissistic gratification and need for stroking.

Most seniors would like to remain independent and free from reliance on their children for support. But as time marches on, this wishful thinking gives way to needs rather than wants. Physical capabilities and confidence makes acceptance of Durable Medical Equipment such as canes, walkers and wheelchairs non-negotiable; likewise, attendants and companions are an imperative for daily living and enjoyment.

The overriding issue in growing old is how well you can make the transition to doing less with less. The damping down of emotional and physical reserves make one more risk-adverse and in search of guard rails that make a daily routine more supportive. In this adjustment you have more free time to obsessively manage your life day-to-day.

Naturally, you pay greater attention to how your organs function. Bowel habits become a monitored event and constipation is a matter of concern. You track the morning stiffness in your joints and back, similarly note the migratory soreness in the muscle bundles in various parts of your anatomy. Minor symptoms such as a runny nose or cough are paid attention to because they might lead to something more serious. When picking up your medications, you begin to read the labels of the OTC preparations that address common complaints such as insomnia, irritable bowel syndrome, indigestion and minor pain. You begin to take note of pharmaceutical ads on TV and social media that offer quick cures. You might impulsively buy a Fitbit to keep track of your sleep scores and pulse rates—when you become addicted to checking these indicators, you upgrade to one that can check your heart rhythm for atrial fibrillation or some other arrhythmia that can be transmitted wirelessly to your healthcare provider for interpretation and advice. With this plethora of real and imagined threats from medical problems, you soon realize that your health is the gatekeeper or intermediary for all of your activities. Psychologists might label this neurotic thinking, but as life expectancy closes in, it reflects normal human survival behavior.

Long trips and overseas travel require greater attention to the details of the itinerary. Considerations include how long will I have to stand in line and are there stairs or hills to climb? Are there restrooms conveniently located and if you need help, are there other members of the party that can assist you? Missing a connecting flight or having car problems are more challenging, so when visiting another distant country you need to check access to adequate medical care. Most importantly, you must make allowances for jet lag that screws with your circadian rhythms. These are things that you probably brushed aside when you were younger and could, if you missed your flight, spend a sleepless night waiting for the next flight without undue stress.

Because most married couples do not develop serious wellness or medical conditions simultaneously, the healthier or more able spouse usually has to assist in his or her partner's care. If both are medically compromised, it becomes a question of who takes care of whom. Who has their car keys taken away first; a millstone that requires the mate or friends to drive to events, shopping and doctor's appointments. Often care needs raise serious questions as to how you reconfigure your house to meet the needs of the disabled partner and safety-proof your home.

Does he or she have problems negotiating the stairs and should you consider a stair lift or even converting a first floor room into a bedroom and the first floor half-bath into a full bath.

These needs are exacerbated if you live alone or lose your loved one. The major consideration often rests with financial means. Can you afford to hire some outside part-time or full-time caregivers and can one or more of your children assume some of the responsibility for needed care. These are lifestyle changing decisions that shatter one's ability to grow old graciously as you traverse the road to dependency.

Allegedly, old folks dote on the past and tend to embellish how things used to be. This favoring of the past over the present is natural as the hard drive of memory within your hippocampus is filled with information from the past. However, I think both long- and short-term memory become suspect at a similar rate even though "senior moments" and blocking on names is usually more prevalent for new names and information. And the good or bad memories seem to hang around after realities change and they are no longer relevant. We certainly remember that first kiss, the first car, a sport's trophy, and graduation as well as the hard knocks of disappointments. As a part of success most of us learn more from our mistakes than our triumphs.

As I age, it seems more and more difficult to conjure up the intensity of feelings I once had for celebrations, reunions, and accomplishments. As an example, the Christmas holidays no longer bring the cheer and luster of earlier times. I think for many elders the repetitious holiday seasons seem like a frenetic inconvenience and intrusion as they rarely meet expectations. On the flip side, it is curious that many simple acts of kindness, outdated expressions your parents used, idiosyncratic personality traits of friends, sage unsolicited advice and random acts of kindness often surface pleasantly and randomly in your conscience thoughts.

Negative occurrences seem more difficult to eradicate than positive ones. In meaningful relationships, one violation of trust is the equivalent of innumerable acts of fidelity. It is a bit like PTSD that lingers in the shadows and colors feelings even as the trauma was transient and in the past with little bearing to the present.

During my college years, like so many other undergraduates, I had a struggle with the dragon of depression. It was painful and the anxiety of that period left its mark. Those feelings color my empathy for others with depression and anxiety and in some ways my experience with depression made me a better caring physician when I was in practice.

I have noticed that many of my elderly high-net-worth friends are quite conservative, tribal, complacent and resistant to entertaining opposing points of views. They are resistant to change. They stay in their comfort zones and avoid discussions about weighty issues. Thus, at the bridge table small talk dominates and you rarely are afforded knowledge about the workings of your bridge friend's points of view.

A number of friends have cemented their legacy with tax-deductible charitable giving especially for naming rights for an academic chair or new building at a well-endowed University or Hospital. I question whether universities and hospitals should be charitable institutions, and in my opinion, even if you do not get legacy recognitions, there are many starved charities where money would have a more profound and humane impact.

One stark reality that attends aging is a new set of athletic signposts on the downward trajectory of your journey. As an example, in club tennis when you are sixty, you usually can avoid being shut out when playing with your children and grandchildren. That ceases to be the case during the next twenty years as you have to abandon singles due to cranky knees, less agility and endurance. Gradually your skill level declines from a USTA 4.5 to 3.5 and your court coverage is just adequate to play competitive doubles with your contemporaries. Further decline relegates you to hitting with the old men and women that hit loopy returns from their static positions. This progression holds true even with less physically demanding sports like golf, walking, bowling, and birding. If golf is your game, you come to believe that the ideal golf course should be 12 holes long rather than 18 and the refreshments should kick in at the 13th hole. Most discouraging is the fact that your drives even off of the gold or ladies tees do not go as far on the fairway as the drives of your grandson who plays golf once a year and drives from the blue tees. You address this differential by focusing on your short game and putting; a rationalization that derives from the old expression "driving is for show; putting is for dough!"

Perhaps the most disturbing parts of the dwindling process is when your visual deficits or multiple fender bender accidents prompts your family to suggest that you give up your driver's license, expensive car insurance and car keys. Your first reaction is often to hide the car keys; but the family often has a plan that goes through your Primary Care Physician who encourages you to take a safety test that has a time limit and which most compromised seniors fail to pass. This leads to a license suspension and there goes your freedom bird. Symbolically, a car in the garage gives you a sense of freedom and dispensing with that convenience is a severe blow to your independence and confidence.

About the same time as your car keys are taken away, suggestions surface that you should consider moving from the family homestead and downsizing into less spacious quarters. This first step to downsize seems reasonable enough especially if you have difficulty navigating stairs and doing routine chores to maintain a two-story home with 2500 square feet. Downsizing sounds simple enough, but for families that have lived many years in the same home and are mild packrats, the distribution of the massive amount of 'stuff' presents a real problem especially if every fixture and artifact tell a story and has some sentimental value. The grown kids have their own 'stuff' and thus you are left with the difficult process of overloading you new digs with your "stuff" and sorting through all of your redundant 'stuff' including tools, paintings, plants, clothes, machines and so on. Making the stressful decisions as to what to throw away, what to give to a charity or place in the Goodwill bin and separating out the items with resale value takes time and effort. Selling your "stuff" is not easy and in desperation with insistence you try to pawn those valuable items off on the kids to add to their "stuff."

Personally, to my way of thinking, the final indignity is when for medical reasons you are persuaded or 'coerced 'into looking for a final placement in a retirement community. These warehouses of humanity offer three levels of residence: independent living, assisted living and nursing home or memory care. This final displacement makes sense but that does not mitigate a feeling of being dumped. Because the average age at which someone applies to a retirement community is 82, the first impression one has when settling into a retirement home is that all those people are so old and predominately women. But there is an upside because if you are still cognitively intact and mobile, then it is relatively easy to make a new circle of friends who play bridge and board games together. If you have a car and can still drive at night, your new social circle expands rapidly.

Economics often drives much of these life changing decisions as your beneficiaries with your feedback contemplate the various options as to what to do with the old folks; that meaning you. Questions such as costs of a home attendant, retirement home placement, apartment rent, condo costs and so on are very real issues. And most importantly your retirement assets heavily factor into these decisions as to what you and yours can afford. All your heirs may be keenly aware of the "inheritance factor."

When couples age together, they commonly do not physically or cognitively age synchronously in locked step. In an uneven fashion each person develops his or her physical limitations. If you wish to remain in your home, this may require a role reversal in which the more capable partner assumes added responsibilities. As a husband, I may have to do the grocery shopping, cooking and laundry, plus activities that require familiarization with a range of home appliances. For a wife, it may include paying the bills, maintaining the budget and getting help with landscaping and yard cleanup. To make these adjustments require sacrifices that alters the social calendar and outside activities. If finances allow, a home care agency can be hired to fill the gaps and free up time for the husband or wife to go about their usual activities. If you have children living close by, they often play an active support role. But medical circumstances make growing "old in place" in your home a time laced with many threats that are difficult to address in a proactive fashion. Last, illness may sink the ship altogether as a mate passes on leaving you alone to reconstruct your remaining years.

Cognitive and physical decline creeps up gradually as you age. It may go unnoticed and early on is easily compensated for in your daily routines. Even if your cognitive skills are in decline; your hard-wired social skills can maintain relationships with a friendly smile, a handshake and simple chatter about the weather and so on. Often only the family appreciates the degree of memory loss that compromises responsible behaviors and imposes a need for surveillance to keep you safe. Only intimate friends and family can detect the subtle changes in affect, lack of interest and withdrawal that usually goes unnoticed in superficial relationships.

Unfortunately, there are few good solutions to the medical classifications of dementia as no medications has been shown to alter the outcome even as some medications are in the pipeline to improve short term memory in Alzheimer's.

The aging brain does not erase the memory of your baseline physical abilities from your youth. Because of this your earlier capabilities tend to act as benchmarks of performance that lead you to agree to activities that challenge the limits of your endurance and strength; not to mention imposing the risks of orthopedic and cardiac complications. If you do not accept your physical limitations, you might sign up for a side trip during a cruise to go jet skiing in the open ocean. You might consider the black diamond ski slopes as doable because they were when you were on the ski team in college. Your physical endurance may be overwhelmed when you take that 8-mile trip through Mammoth Cave that entails many hundreds of steps. Unfortunately, just one or two of these miscalculations bring you down to earth and causes that epiphany that aligns your impulses with reality. If you excelled at something like tennis or golf as a youth; this process to tamp down expectations is disheartening.

Senior moments of forgetting names and past activities are universal at any age. The question that is commonly discussed is how many senior moments, forgot to attend moments and neglect of simple matters imply some sort of cognitive impairment. There is no good answer and one can always harp back to being them "absent minded professor" to rationalize our forgetfulness. But senior moments are a greater concern to seniors because they raise a hint of cognitive decline and the need for reassurance that this does not foreshadow dementia.

One of the most disturbing features of the declining years is how things in the past that used to give you intense pleasure no longer stir the same degree of passion. Even sexual feelings that once were omnipresent in your chain of thought lack the oomph and desire as in earlier days. Sexual performance, if still an option, takes more encouragement to initiate and effort to consummate with an experience that lacks the ecstasy of earlier days.

Accessing old family movies and picture albums conjure up fond memories of the past. However, after one viewing, they often just gather dust on the shelf. I had our 16 mm family movies dating back to the 1930s converted to DVDs and then to voice-over-video to preserve them for posterity. Young family members enjoy viewing them once and show enough interest to download them into their computers where they probably will linger and become forgotten with the advent of new technology. Unlike in many other cultures, our rapid-pace society with information overload does not tend to obsess on family history or any form of ancestor worship. A recent renewed interest in genetics from sites like "23 and me" has stimulated interest in where your ancestor's DNA originated but that is not the same as giving you a feel for how it was to live in those times. Family letters and other artifacts are more revealing. In the future, however, from a medical perspective a complete genetic analysis may carry real significance with regard to addressing and mitigating ones' risk factors for disease.

Loneliness is an insidious feature of growing old. Your children and grandchildren who you dearly love and who dearly love you are busy with their own lives. They visit, but that must dovetail into their schedule. But owning the family business, having a broad network of influential friends or a large estate can be a magnet in your relationships with your children. But when incapacity and infirmity strike, you may become more of a burden and puzzle as to what to do with the old folks. The issues come into greater focus when a partner dies. When death steals a mate, the statistics show that women seem to adjust better to living alone than men. Their longevity is also greater, and men seem to have a greater propensity to get remarried; often to younger women who end up being caregivers.

In 1967, the Age Discrimination in Employment Act (ADEA) was passed that applied to individual over the "young" age of 40. This may cover employment, but age discrimination for true seniors is more subtle. Most young individuals feel kindly and more considerate of old folks. They open doors; let you go first; offer their seats and assist with heavy lifting. However, chronological age and the wrinkles of time mitigate the options offered to capable, experienced seniors. Older folks generally make the newspaper only if they give a large donation to charity or do something extraordinary that is linked to their longevity.

Transferrable wealth may alter the equation as even old rich nasty curmudgeons that I have known have been coddled and tolerated because of their affluence.

Because many seniors have inadequate retirement funds and cannot live on social security alone, the need arises to find some type of gainful employment. Here their former work experience rarely commands a living wage. Nonprofits boards and volunteers are essentially unpaid positions even as nonprofits actively recruit volunteers with legal, accounting and marketing skills. Consciously, unconsciously, or realistically, aging is equated to declining performance. But often seniors have unique skills that are overlooked. Some professions such as law and medicine enable some to continue to practice long after the age 65, the supposed threshold of retirement.

It is often said that there are no atheists "when fighting in the trenches." The last chapter in life causes a greater awareness of your mortality and because of this, older folks tend to become more religious and conscientious about attending church services. Humans have a profound need for metaphysical purpose with the expectation of some form of life after death. But to my way of thinking science challenges a belief in heaven and paradise. I believe that life is a gift, and that we live in a beautifully world with miraculous features. The human body is a perfect example of incredible engineering that could only come from a supreme being. But do humans have souls that carry us into the afterworld? It is comforting to think so but individually, I have not witnessed any interaction with the supernatural. I envy those, like my Mother, that through faith believe in the afterlife.

Moreover, it is highly doubtful that we are alone in the universe. The Webb Telescope that confirms the presences of billions of galaxies just like the Milky Way which is a million light years across strongly suggests that there are billions of other planets and celestial bodies with life forms. Other civilizations may be chemically different and have different shapes, but, in my opinion, it is naïve to think that we are alone. Even with unexplained UFOs sighting, it is doubtful that we have been visited by alien visitors because the closest star is 4 light years away.

In some free verse that I wrote several years ago I stated, "And accept aging as an investment in maturity." This is a delightful rationalization, but I admit it is far from the truth. Experience and a life of hard knocks many have some survival insights but does not necessarily give you special knowledge or wisdom. Despite my advanced age, I do not have a good answer as to the meaning of life other than each of us has a unique journey and with a little bit of luck and advantage you will enjoy the ride and express your full potential. In the Maslow Hierarchy of Needs Model you may come close to achieving self-actualization.

Lists become more important as you age; unfortunately they are the list of chronic disorders, prescription meds and medical specialist appointments as opposed to shopping lists, meetings and entertainments. When it comes to diseases, you hope none are fatal and that good treatments with tolerable side effects exist to hold them in check for a while. Heading most lists of disorders is degenerative arthritis that causes pain and stiffness but is not generally fatal even as it impairs your mobility, balance and strength. Many maladies do not make the list because they creep up over many years like sarcopenia (muscle weakness), osteopenia (weak bones), easy fatigability, 10-20 decibel hearing loss, cataracts, getting up at nights to pass water, less ambition and a desire to hibernate and do nothing. To counter these intruders you develop a fatalistic melancholy about joys that will never come again.

This nostalgic sadness that centers on the beauty of life and living produces a low-grade euphoric love of where you have been and an acceptance of mortality.

Perhaps the most difficult part of the journey is seeing that all the things you love, cherish and delight in disappear over time. As a Chinese philosopher observed; "everything you have you lose." It is hard to see family members, colleagues and friends fade and die, move and change and disappear as confidants with whom you shared feelings and ideas. It is the sadness in life that makes us appreciate life. One philosopher conjectured that "the leaving of somethings is the appreciation of that thing." I know I appreciate the good things in the past even as they will never come again. Nostalgia, empathy and loss are the matrix of life as you grow old and perhaps the appreciation and gratefulness of having lived so long and so well.

It seems strange that at a time in life where social circles are shrinking, that older folks like me do not reach out to old friends and acquaintances to retain some semblance of active social engagement. I have many friends I could contact, but neglect to do so. It is especially sad because so many live alone with limited family support. Reaching out could brighten their spirits and help fight depression.

Perhaps I should keep a list of friends with whom I have shared interests and call on a regular basis. I know that getting an unexpected call from an old friend brightens the day. If you downsize or are forced into a retirement community with unfamiliar surroundings and a new circle of folks, you must make the effort to reach out and connect. Granted, when you arrive and sit down for your first evening meal, your impression is that there are too many old people with flat affect here. Get over it and connect; you are often surprised at their needs to be friendly and share their remarkable journeys with you.

Yearly, we typically take a cruise with our family originating in Fort Lauderdale to the Bahamas. Cruises afford an escape from the winter cold. Most itineraries offer a host of side trips and excursions. One problem is that these humongous cruise ship that weigh 150,000 tons or more are moored at docks that are almost a half mile long. Additionally, with multiple ships in the same port, it produces a chaotic crush of sightseers eager to shop, explore and board tour busses. The pools, hot tubs, and water parks on the ship draw a raucous and intoxicated crowd and the massive water slides are daunting and scary for seniors. Thus the main attraction for this senior is putt-putt golf, board games, the casino, spa, shows and so on. Of course, the array of food is the central focus and this, of course, causes you to gain several pounds if not more. However, at the end of the day, cruises are probably the most relaxing, stress free and affordable type of vacations for senior citizens. Best of all, if you go with family, it offers a marvelous time together from which the grandchildren cannot escape.

If you have the luxury of having a bunch of offspring who love you and want the best for you, you often find that some of the kids unfortunately do not get along with one another. Even through you may be very needy, you can still act as a catalyst to bring the tribe together. You can arrange lunches, suggest positive family function and jointly craft your will with them in a way that minimizes conflict after you are gone. In my experience, nothing is more disruptive to a family than having members who feel cheated in the distribution of their parent's wealth. Crafting a fair will, of course, is not easy; some members of the family have moved away and are not involved in your day to day life or care and some are not as well off as others. Moreover you may have a favorite or be angry for one reason or another and threaten to give all of your assets to a favorite charity. My advice is that your Will should be a consensus building exercise; think on it.

Finally, if possible, I think it is challenging to die with dignity and reverence. The end of your stay can bring serenity to your loved ones if you are grateful for their gifts and you are grateful for the privilege to have lived and been with them.

At the end of the day, growing old is a learning exercise to do less with less and graciously accept and adapt to you shrinking range of options. Which I might add is a personal hope that I will present another paper to this august group in 2-3 years from now.

DICK WENDEL is a retired physician (urologist) with an Executive MBA from Xavier University. He volunteers as a SCORE counselor and as a moderator for classes on medical subjects at OLLI (senior learning at the University of Cincinnati). He is also author of *Retire with a Mission* published by SourceBooks.

16

Madame X

JAMES WESNER

You can still see her if you go to the basement at the Metropolitan Museum of Art in New York and ask a curator to pull out the sliding panel on which her portrait is mounted. But the crabbed viewing in the storage area does not replicate the effect produced when she reigned in the grand space at the entrance to the Museum's American Wing, beckoning the viewer to enter and enjoy the many pleasures within.

Our mind's eye sees her in her former prominence as she stands erect, framed in a plain but elegant gold rectangle, her body turned toward us in a frontal pose, her right hand resting on a small table carved with sirens, her left grasping the fabric of her gown. The gown is black, highlighted to show fold in the fabric, the waist is narrow, the bodice ample, and the shoulders bare; the whole ensemble is supported by two narrow straps that do not appear equal to the task. Her head is turned in profile, revealing a sharp Gallic nose, accompanied by compressed lips, half closed eyes, and raised eyebrows that together produce the effect of haughty self-assurance. A tiny tiara shaped like a crescent moon, the symbol of Diana, crowns her upswept, henna-washed hair. Her figure stands out sharply against a dull grey-green background, which contrasts with the pale lavender tint of the cosmetic powder she applied to her face, arms, and shoulders. The natural color of her unpowdered ear startles as it reveals the artifice. What we see is a very beautiful woman, attracting like a siren yet as unapproachable as Diana, the trophy wife of Pierre Gautreau, a rich Parisian banker twice her age.

Virginie Amélie Avegno Gautreau was born in New Orleans on 29 January 1859. Her family owned Parlange, a large sugar plantation located in Pointe Coupée Parish north of Baton Rouge. Her father, a colonel in the Confederate Army, was killed at Shiloh in

1862. In 1867, when Virginie was eight, her widowed mother moved with her to Paris, where she was educated and introduced to society. Virginie soon became one of high society's celebrated beauties and, with her marriage to Pierre Gautreau, gained the means and connections that facilitated her continued climb in the whirl of Parisian high society. She was what Parisians called a "professional beauty," meaning one who rose in society through skillful use of her looks and wits. And, like many of the type, her ascent was accompanied by rumors of sexual adventures that titillated but did not wander over the line into disqualifying scandal.

John Singer Sargent, the son of American expats headquartered in Paris, was born in Florence, Italy, on 12 January 1856. His parents' peregrinations around Europe gave him a solid knowledge of European history and art and the ability to speak fluent English, French, Italian, and German. After receiving his diploma from l' École des Beaux-Arts in Paris, Sargent began a career in Paris as a portrait artist and landscape painter, exhibiting successfully at the Paris Exhibitions of 1879, 1880 and 1881. Like many others, Sargent became infatuated with the beauty and glittering social life of Madame Gautreau and asked a mutual friend to help persuade her to let him paint her portrait. Although she had refused others, she accepted his offer. He did the work without a commission, meaning Sargent would own the resulting portrait—a fact of consequence in light of future events.

The work on the portrait began in November 1883, but Virginie was a poor sitter and matters went slowly. Sargent was invited to spend the summer with the family at their summer place in Saint-Malo, Brittany, where the work continued into the fall, in the process producing about 30 drawings in pen and ink, pastels, watercolors and oils. By fall, the finished portrait was ready. Sargent's hope was that it would help him gain lucrative commissions by making a splash at the Exhibition of 1884. To ensure his work would be noticed, his entry was full length to dominate the wall space where it would hang. More publicity might be expected by the subject, whose identity would be thinly disguised by a title that would fool no one.

Seldom in the history of art has there been a greater miscalculation. When the Exhibition opened, great crowds gathered around the portrait, which originally had been painted with the right strap dangling loosely over Virginie's bare shoulder. It certainly looked as if her gown was about to come off, although it was in fact supported by a wire cage, and it was obvious there could be no petticoat under the bodice. Her pose, based on classical models, appeared not chaste but provocative when combined with the décolleté gown, and the use of body powder appeared artificial and false. Although there were many classical nudes in the Exhibition, Madame X was the sexiest picture there, and not at all in a good way. What Virginie had thought the height of fashion was deemed risqué by the gentlemen and vulgar by the ladies. And the critics hated it, lambasting the "pallor" of the subject's skin and the indecency of her pose. The reviewer from Le Figaro, commenting on the dangling strap, said, "One more struggle, and the lady will be free."

A modern art historian has suggested that the outrage the portrait inspired may be attributed in part to the difference between Madame Gautreau seen in motion, perceived by most as beautiful, and her image fixed on canvass in a single pose, where her physical and moral faults were exposed. The overuse of cosmetics, the over-haughty expression, the too deep cleavage are there for all to see, but would not be so evident in the living, moving woman. At any rate, the portrait does not provoke the same negative reactions in the modern viewer—or at least not in this modern viewer. What I see is a striking portrait, evocative of the Belle Epoque, yet unlike the standard portrayal of an upper-class woman. She is beautiful, of course, but there is more: woman as an imagined ideal, commanding, attracting, unattainable. It is this, I believe, that has made the painting so popular in later ages.

Faced with the disastrous public reaction, Virginie and her mother went to Sargent in tears and begged him to withdraw the portrait. He refused, telling them he had painted what she chose to wear. What Pierre's position was in all of this is not reported. When the Exhibition closed, Sargent went early to remove it himself to make sure the family did not try to destroy it. He painted over the dangling strap with an upright one and kept the portrait on prominent display in his studio for the next 32 years. At first, he refused to lend it to exhibitions, but relented in 1905 and allowed its public display at the Carfax Gallery in London and in several subsequent international art shows.

A few critics reviewing the 1884 Exhibition had kind words for Sargent's "cosmopolitism," but the hostile consensus was a disaster for the young artist's ambitions. Since his prospects for commissions in Paris had evaporated with the scandal, he moved to London in 1885 and rapidly gained the English and American commissions denied him in Paris. Sargent died in London on 14 April 1925, leaving behind a reputation as the leading portrait painter of the Edwardian Age.

As the portrait of Virginie Amélie Avegno Gautreau slides back into its assigned slot, the aphorism "Everyone is entitled to 15 minutes of fame" comes to mind. Madame Gautreau did better than that. She survived the scandal and was later painted by two other prominent artists, one of whom, Gustave Courtois, portrayed her in 1891 wearing a low-cut dress with one strap hanging off her shoulder in the same profile pose as had Sargent. However, times had changed, and his painting was praised. Virginie died on 25 July 1915 and was buried in the family vault at her summer home in Saint-Malo, where she and Sargent had worked on the infamous portrait so many years before. Pierre, anonymous to the end, survived her.

In 1916, Sargent offered to sell Madame X to the Metropolitan Museum of Art for £1,000, or about $140,000 in today's money. In his offer letter, he said, "I suppose it is the best thing I have ever done." And, despite a long and distinguished career that extended into the twenties, most art critics today agree that Madame X is indeed his masterpiece.

JIM WESNER is a recovering redneck who was born north of Shreveport, Louisiana, but grew up in New Orleans and hopes you will forget the Shreveport part. Long retired from his last job as General Counsel of the University of Cincinnati, Jim amuses himself with reading and writing about history, art and literature.